Celia

A Slave

MELTON A. McLAURIN

Perennial

An Imprint of HarperCollinsPublishers

HarperCollins books may be purchased for educational, business, or sales promotional use. For information, please e-mail the Special Markets Department at SPsales@harpercollins.com.

First Avon Books edition published 1993.

Reprinted in Perennial 2002.

The Library of Congress has catalogued the hardcover edition as follows:
McLaurin, Melton Alonza.
    Celia, a slave / Melton A. McLaurin.
        p. cm.
Includes bibliographical references and index.
    1. Celia, d. 1855—trials, litigation, etc.. 2. Trials (Murder)—Missouri—Callaway County. 3. Slavery—Southern States—Moral conditions.
I. Title.
KF223.C43M34   1991
345.73'02523—dc20   90-23045
[347.3052523]   CIP

ISBN 0-380-71935-5 (pbk.)

    18 19 ♦/LSC 40 39 38 37 36

To Sandra
in admiration of her
courage and conviction

Acknowledgments

As an academic discipline, history possesses an inherent tension, one that every historian confronts. On the one hand, history is the study of the recorded past, of data, of facts. At times the record is dry and dull, at others, as with the case examined in this work, the record holds the power to captivate. History is also the search for the meaning of the recorded past, an interpretation of data, an exploration of the significance of facts. It is the effort to interpret, to explain, that distinguishes the historian from the storyteller. Yet historians ignore their role as storytellers to their peril, if they wish to address an audience beyond the academy, to enter into a meaningful dialogue with the larger society.

This work represents an attempt to resolve that tension, or at least to bring it to bear upon the effort to know and to understand a portion of the American past. Several colleagues graciously offered advice about how to do this most effectively. Comments from Robert Hall of Northeastern University; Jacqueline Goggin of Clark University; Peter Stead of Swansea College, University of Wales; Gary Kremer of the Missouri State Archives; and Kathleen Berkeley of the University of North Carolina at Wilmington were especially helpful. So, too, were the comments of readers for the University of Georgia Press. For the advice received, and for the time and energy devoted to reading the work in manuscript, I am truly grateful.

Contents

Contents

Introduction

The lives of public figures, those whom society comes to regard as great men and women, are often used by historians and biographers to exemplify or define an issue or era from the past. In the mid-nineteenth century, for example, Elizabeth Cady Stanton came to represent the women's movement; Frederick Douglass and William Lloyd Garrison the abolitionists; Dorothea Dix reform in the treatment of the criminal and the insane; Edmund Ruffin and William Loundes Yancey a fierce southern nationalism based upon the defense and perpetuation of the institution of slavery. Yet the lives of lesser figures, men and women who lived and died in virtual anonymity, often better illustrate certain aspects of the major issues of a particular period than do the lives of those who, through significant achievement, the appeal of the orator, or the skill of the polemicist, achieve national prominence.

Such is the case with the life of Celia, a slave who lived and died in Callaway County, Missouri. On October 9, 1855,

Celia entered the circuit court of Callaway County, where she stood accused of murder. Approximately nineteen years of age and already the mother of two children, the accused was defended by a team of three lawyers. The most prominent of her defense attorneys was a popular figure in the county seat of Fulton, a man who had been three times elected to serve his constituents in the United States Congress. Celia's trial, its causes and consequences, confront us with the hard daily realities of slavery rather than with the abstract theories about the workings of that institution so carefully developed and explored by historians in the last quarter-century.

Celia's life, like any life, cannot give us a complete understanding of an institution so complex as slavery. Its ability to inform us is limited by the fact that the record of Celia's life, like that of most lives judged inconsequential, is incomplete. Since the significance of Celia's story rests in large part upon the manner in which others responded to her, the gaps in the historical record only underscore the historian's difficulty in assessing the motives of those individuals, of determining intent. Assumptions are employed to fill these gaps. Such assumptions are based upon a careful consideration of the record extant, of the historical backdrop against which the events of Celia's life played out, and of the past quarter-century of scholarship on slavery. Celia's life also informs us little about certain aspects of slavery, for example the political economy of slavery, or the structure and activities of the slave community. Nor does it inform us about the complex political and constitutional issues to which slavery gave rise, and which ultimately disrupted the union.

Rather, the life of Celia, a slave, presents us with a detailed case study of what the historian Charles Sellers referred to as "the fundamental moral anxiety" that slavery produced. This fundamental moral anxiety, and the moral dilemmas that produced it, were at the very heart of the institution of slavery. Until recently they have received little attention from historians, who concentrated instead upon the economic and social aspects of slavery, and upon the political issues it created. For many antebellum southerners, including the large majority who held no slaves, the moral dilemmas of slavery were hardly abstractions to be debated. They were instead among the inescapable realities of daily life, a significant aspect of the society. And as such southerners, slaveholders or not, were forced to cope with them in terms of the concrete, rather than the theoretical. These same moral dilemmas, and the moral anxiety they produced, were equally crucial to, and unavoidable in, the political struggles that eventually led to the Civil War.[1]

The life of Celia demonstrates how slavery placed individuals, black and white, in specific situations that forced them to make and to act upon personal decisions of a fundamentally moral nature. Such decisions involved, and inevitably affected, the lives of both the decision maker and the individuals caught in the moral dilemma about which decisions were made. Ultimately, each of these individual decisions was also a judgment about the morality of the institution of slavery itself. The events of Celia's life, and the decisions they forced upon others, also forcefully remind us that personal decisions about the morality of slavery were never made in a social and political vacuum. Individual responses to the moral dilemmas posed by slavery were inevitably linked to the political issue of slavery within the larger society, especially during periods when the peculiar institution was under attack.[2]

Celia's story derives much of its significance, as well as its narrative power, from the nature of the specific issues and moral dilemmas it forced individuals to confront. Her case starkly reveals the relationships of race, gender, and power in the antebellum South, in addition to illustrating the manner in which the law was employed to assuage the moral anxiety slavery produced. Finally, because race and gender are issues with which our society continues to grapple, and because both remain major factors in the distribution of power within modern society, the case of Celia, a slave, reminds us that the personal and the political are never totally separate entities.

One

Beginnings

Robert Newsom seemed the ideal representative of the family farmers who in 1850 composed the majority of the citizens of Callaway County, Missouri. His life experiences, family relationships, and economic status made him seem so. Indeed, nothing in the public record indicated that Robert Newsom was anything other than what he seemed—a man who had labored hard and endured much for the measure of prosperity he had achieved; a good father who continued to contribute to the welfare of his children, all now themselves adults; a man who had gained the respect of his neighbors. In many respects he was the fulfillment of the Jeffersonian dream, the personification of the ideals that had led to the purchase of the territory in which he settled. He was, as were so many of his fellow Missourians, the self-sufficient yeoman farmer, secure because of the abundance that came from the land he owned, and which he helped to till.

The journey of Robert Newsom and his family to Missouri had been typical of that undertaken by many of his fellow

1

citizens of Callaway County. His was among the many families to abandon Virginia in the second decade of the nineteenth century and trek westward to the newly created territories of the transmontane southwest. The promise of a better life took the Newsoms to Missouri sometime between 1819 and 1822. Like thousands of others who were fleeing the overcropped lands of the east, the Newsoms recognized the potential of the rich river bottom lands of the most recent addition to the Union. Robert had made his westward journey with his wife, whose name we do not know, and son Harry and daughter Virginia, both of whom were born in Virginia. The method by which they traveled is unknown, but however they traveled it would have been an arduous journey for the family, and not without danger, especially for the children. Virginia would have been an infant, at most not more than two years of age; Harry would have been no more than seven. The rigors of travel on the western frontier would have exposed both children to accident and disease, whether the family journeyed overland through Kentucky or took the more likely route by flatboat down the Ohio and Mississippi to the burgeoning river port of St. Louis.[1]

If they entered the territory from St. Louis, it is probable that Robert Newsom took his young family up the Missouri, a notoriously difficult river to navigate. Although European and American settlers had used the river for decades, until the second decade of the nineteenth century such traffic was haphazardly organized and risky in the extreme. Canoes and pirogues, often rafted in pairs, were frequently used on the river, as were mackinaws, flat-bottomed, high-prowed craft capable of only downriver voyages, and skinboats, flimsy, unstable craft made of buffalo hide that deteriorated rapidly. Keelboats were introduced to the Big Muddy only in 1811, when rival fur-trading companies launched expeditions on a race upstream on high spring waters. Not until 1819, two years after they appeared in St. Louis on the Mississippi, did steamboats ascend the Missouri.

At the time the Newsom family arrived in Missouri, all of these craft were still used on the river. If the family went inland on its waters, their financial situation would have determined the craft in which they traveled. Quite possibly the family ascended the river by steamboat, although such travel would have been expensive, as the fur company boats remained the only such vessels on the river. Chances are that the family traveled by keelboat, their vessel powered by muscular rivermen, some of whom may have plied their trade since the great race that inaugurated keelboat service on the Missouri. Although less likely, the Newsoms may have come upriver in a solid, serviceable pirogue, hewn from a single walnut or cottonwood log, their provisions strewn about its bottom, protected from hungry river rats by a cat or two.[2]

Regardless of their mode of travel, by the fall of 1822 Robert Newsom and his family had settled in southern Callaway County, in a section that would eventually become Fulton Township. The Newsom family was but one of many to immigrate to the region after lands there were opened for sale to the public in December 1818. Like many early settlers, Robert Newsom selected land along the timbered shores of a river or creek, a site that provided rich alluvial soils for crops, wood for building and for fuel, and an inexpensive means of transporting the crops he planned to raise and the products he hoped to purchase from the profits his sale of the harvest would bring. The site Newsom purchased was located on the Middle River, a minor tributary of the Missouri, some nine miles south of the locality that would eventually become the town of Fulton.[3]

The Newsoms and their neighbors, who settled the farmlands along the banks of the Middle River, had come to Missouri in pursuit of prosperity and the more rewarding

3

life they hoped prosperity would bring. Theirs was a dream both unique and common, individual and communal. Most, like the Newsoms, came from Virginia and North Carolina, a few from New York, Pennsylvania, and other northern states of the eastern seaboard. A surprising number came from Kentucky and Tennessee, the first of the transmontane states to send their restless citizenry further west in the relentless American pursuit of happiness. They had come on the rivers by keel and flatboat, in canoes and dugouts, on rafts of roughsawed planking nailed across fresh-cut logs. Overland they had come by cart and wagon, astride horses and mules. Many journeyed by foot, plodding mile after mile along widened footpaths that hardly deserved to be called roads. Seekers and dreamers all, they hoped to reach the western promised land, a land said to flow with milk and honey, a land such as their God had promised, and delivered, to the ancient Israelites.

They arrived in a land still untamed, an unbroken wilderness filled with opportunity and danger. Early settlers of south Callaway County found the first years hard, despite the fertility of the land. Even basic supplies proved difficult to obtain, and the county's new residents imported bread and other staples from Fort Cooper in Howard County, a supply depot upriver that could be reached only after a journey of several days. Salt, an essential item, was transported overland from Boone's Lick, a distance of forty miles. Basic rations had to be supplemented with game killed in the woodlands. Luckily, the territory's virgin forest teemed with game large and small—elk and deer, wild turkeys, ducks, and squirrels. While some forest creatures supplied meat for the settlers' tables, others threatened the newcomers' efforts to tame the land. Poisonous snakes, especially rattlesnakes, were abundant, posing a serious danger to settlers. Snakebite, a constant threat during warm weather, inevitably resulted in serious illness and sometimes death. The swine, cattle, and sheep brought into the region by settlers faced a different threat as they foraged in the woodlands. Bears, wolves, and panthers that prowled the forests took a heavy toll on the county's early livestock herds. So numerous and threatening were these predators that in 1824 some Callaway settlers created a common fund, agreeing to pay a bushel of corn for each animal scalp or pelt hunters presented. The frontiersmen responded to the challenge, killing hundreds of animals. On the day appointed they surrendered their furs and received their payment. It was, according to an early settler of the region, a memorable event, and only after "indulging in a great fandango of fun and frolic" did the hunters and their families, perhaps including the family of Robert Newsom, return to their homes.[4]

Gradually the people of south Callaway County subdued the wilderness, claiming by the sweat of their brows their individual piece of the Canaan President Jefferson had purchased for them, keeping faith with his dream. They cleared the forest with broadax and fire. They broke the newly cleared ground, littered with roots and stumps, with wooden "Bull plows." Once the land was cleared and prepared, they planted and cultivated their crops, and began to reap the fruits of their labor in the fields they had created. As their herds of livestock grew and their cleared land expanded, Callaway's pioneering residents began the business of establishing the institutions of a settled society, of replicating the older communities of the east which they had so recently abandoned. Religious congregations were among the first institutions formed, and they would first meet in private homes: Baptists, Methodists, Cumberland Presbyterians. Militia units were organized and twice yearly general musters quickly became gala social events, a time for horse-racing, fistfighting, hard drinking and the telling of tall tales. School teachers arrived and set about the task of educating the youngest of the region's new citizens. The people, or rather the men, of the community also began the task of self-government and political organization, of creating a body politic from a collection of individuals of varied origins, all of whom shared a common vision of the future. Robert Newsom was one of those who accepted the duties of citizenship in this emerging society, casting his first ballot in his adopted state in the 1822 elections.[5]

The large majority of those who settled central Missouri, like Robert Newsom, made their living from the land. Most were small farmers, growing a variety of grain crops, with most of their acreage devoted to the production of oats and corn, although some grew substantial amounts of wheat and rye. Grains were supplemented by several other food crops, especially Irish potatoes. Callaway County farmers also soon established large livestock herds, as would Robert Newsom. By 1840, the county's farmers raised herds of swine totaling over 30,000 animals and tended more than 11,000 head of cattle. They tended their farms with the labor of some 7,000 mules and horses and sold the wool produced by nearly 14,000 sheep.[6]

Although the settlers of Callaway County found the prosperity they sought, theirs was the prosperity of the common man. Their settlements were representative of both the biblical ideal of every man in his own vineyard, beneath his own fig tree, and the economic democracy of the American frontier, which would soon find a national symbol in Andrew Jackson. Their original homes were log cabins, ribbed with poles and covered with boards split from trees, floored with rough-hewn planks, with holes two-feet square cut into the walls to serve as windows. Callaway was never a land of huge plantations and grand manors. A pattern of a diversified subsistence agriculture conducted on small family farms rapidly emerged in Callaway County. This pattern, of which the Newsom farm would become representative, discouraged the development of large plantations and the production of cash crops. In 1840, Callaway farmers produced less than 300 tons of hemp, no cotton, and only about 195 tons of tobacco. Although tobacco was by far the county's most important cash crop, it seemed almost insignificant when compared to the 1840 production of more than 1,700,000 pounds in Boone County, which also bordered the Missouri and was Callaway's neighbor to the west. The wool produced by the county's large herds of sheep contributed to the subsistence economy, and provided local farmers with their other source of cash income. The herds also represented an additional source of meat for the settlers' tables. The pattern of small, subsistence family farms so evident in the 1840 census remained unchanged a decade later, as did the agricultural commodities these farms produced.[7]

One historian's examination of a random sample of landowners selected from the county's 1850 census records provides perhaps the best available overview of the economic and social setting in which the family of Robert Newsom lived and worked. The results of this examination reveal a portrait of the "typical" Callaway County farm. The sample was comprised of 179 slaveholders and 120 nonslaveholders, for slaveholding, more than any other factor, distinguished between the county's landholders. The average slaveholder's farm was valued at $1,720, the average nonslaveholder's was valued at less than a third of that figure at $500. The differential between slaveholders and nonslaveholders also is strikingly evident in the productivity of their farms in practically every other category measured, including value of farm implements, livestock, and homemade manufactures. Slaveholders produced on average three times the wheat produced by nonslaveholders, and twice as much corn. Slaveowners held twice as many horses and sheep as did nonslaveholders, and three times as many cattle.

While this differential in productivity between farmers who held slaves and those who did not is evident throughout the

7

sample, even more apparent is the small size of all farms, those of slaveholders and nonslaveholders alike. On average, slaveholders owned slightly more than three hundred acres, of which less than a hundred acres was tended. Nonslaveholders held on average slightly more than a hundred acres, of which but 33 were tended. Thus throughout the antebellum era, while Callaway County's promise to settlers such as Robert Newsom of a better life in a relatively egalitarian white society was fulfilled, it would have been obvious to Newsom and others that the promise was more amply fulfilled for those who held slaves than for those who did not.[8]

The promise and its fulfillment drew a steady stream of seekers to join the Newsom family in their search for prosperity in Callaway County. By 1830 some 6,159 souls were settled on the land—4,702 whites, 1,456 black slaves, and a lone free black. Within the next decade the county's population practically doubled as settlers in ever-increasing numbers fled the overcropped and eroded lands of the eastern seaboard states. In 1840 the county's population totaled 11,765, of whom 8,601 were white and 3,142 were black slaves. Ten years later the county contained 13,827 people, 9,895 of whom were white.[9]

As the county's population increased, as its agricultural productivity quickened and its governmental institutions were put into place, the need for a town to serve as a commercial and political center became apparent. And so, in 1825, at a location some nine miles north of the Newsom farm, a new town was laid out in a wilderness clearing. Men dressed in buckskin pants, shirts, and moccasins traveled distances of up to ten miles on foot to help create the town. In a single day they erected its first building, a log cabin in which they danced that very night. Fulton, the newly created county seat, developed even more rapidly than did the farmland that surrounded it. Before the end of the decade it boasted grocers and saloonkeepers, saddlers and tailors, blacksmiths and merchants, laborers and lawyers. In addition to its county governmental offices and its commercial enterprises, Fulton witnessed the founding of its first religious institution, a Baptist church. In 1827 the fledgling congregation welcomed a new minister, Theodorick Boulware. Boulware, a hard-driving young Virginian like Robert Newsom, was determined to advance both the Baptist version of Christianity and his own personal fortune.[10]

The passing decades were as kind to Robert Newsom. As the summer of 1855 approached, Newsom had reason to be pleased with his decision to make his home in Callaway County. He had become a prosperous man, the owner of some eight hundred acres, almost half of which was improved land, worth some thirty-five hundred dollars according to the 1850 census. His prosperity could also be measured by the crops he produced: wheat, rye, corn and oats, more than twelve hundred bushels of grain per year. The herds of livestock that grazed his pastures, too, gave evidence of his prosperity: eighteen horses, six milch cows, twenty-seven beef cattle, seventy swine, twenty-five sheep and two oxen, with a combined value of approximately one thousand dollars. Although he was not among the county's elite, Newsom's holdings placed him solidly amid the ranks of Callaway's residents who were comfortably well-off.[11]

Included in the goods and property of Robert Newsom in 1850 were five male slaves, for he, like many of his Callaway neighbors, had invested in human chattel. While it is impossible to determine whether he suffered any misgivings, any pangs of conscience over this form of property, it is unlikely that he was greatly troubled by a sense of guilt. He had grown to adulthood in the slaveholding society of Virginia, where slave ownership had long been a mark of social position. The laws of the land condoned the practice, and those of his adopted state encouraged it. Many of his fellow Missourians, especially those who resided in counties such as Callaway that bordered the Missouri River, held slaves. Many such slaveholders believed the institution was justified by the laws of man and of God. While it is possible that Newsom harbored some moral ambiguity about slave ownership, it is far more likely that he regarded it as a fitting reward for his years of labor, an indication of the social status he had achieved through his own efforts.[12]

Robert Newsom's family, too, had prospered. Harry, forty-two in 1855, had acquired a farm of his own, nearly 250 acres, just down the road from his father's place. Despite his prosperity, Harry had encountered personal hardship. His first wife, Jenina Caldwell, had died in 1842, at a time when he was still living with his father. A decade later Harry remarried, taking Miranda Griggs as his wife and leaving his father's household. David, the youngest son, who turned twenty-two in 1855, had married Marry Ann Durham in April of that year. He, too, had moved to his own farm, probably obtained with help from Robert. Like that of his father and brother, David's farm was located in Callaway's Fulton Township.[13]

In 1855, Robert's older daughter, the thirty-six-year-old Virginia, still lived with her father, for what reasons we do not know. She had been married and retained her husband's family name, Waynescot. She had been living with her father at least since 1850, when she appears on the census rolls as a resident in his household. The most logical conclusion is that her husband had died and Virginia had returned with her children to live with her father. In fact, Virginia functioned as the mistress of the Newsom home, for her mother had died sometime in 1849.[14]

Virginia brought her three children from her marriage to Waynescot to reside with their grandfather. James Coffee, the oldest, was approximately twelve years old in the summer of

1855. Amelia, the sole Waynescot girl, was approximately six years old, and Thomas, about nine. A younger child, Billy, was four years old, and presents something of a puzzle since his birth came after a husbandless Virginia moved into her father's home sometime prior to 1850. Rounding out the Robert Newsom household was Mary, Robert's youngest, who at nineteen would have been regarded as an adult in what remained an essentially frontier society.[15]

There was, however, another resident on the Newsom farm, one whose presence reflected the growing prosperity of Robert Newsom. She was the slave Celia, who, when she arrived in 1850, was approximately fourteen years old, about the same age as Newsom's daughter Mary. Practically nothing is known about Celia's life before her arrival at the Newsom farm. Immediately prior to her arrival, she had lived in Audrain County, which borders Callaway to the north. Whether she had been the property of a farmer or planter, or of a resident of Mexico or one of the county's other small towns, is not known, nor is it known if she were born in Audrain County, or how many masters she had before becoming the property of Robert Newsom. Perhaps she had received some training as a cook, for that is one of the duties she performed for the Newsom household.[16]

The prosperity enjoyed by the Newsom family was typical of the booming agricultural economy of Callaway County in 1855. Located on the northern banks of the Missouri River almost exactly in the center of the state, Callaway had by the 1850s become one of Missouri's most prosperous counties. Because it had remained a land of family farms, rather than large plantations, and produced such a wide variety of food crops, its economy was less subject to yearly fluctuations than were the economies of those regions of the state that depended on the major cash crops of hemp, cotton, and tobacco. The large herds of sheep and swine that grazed its pastures and foraged in its woodlands, combined with the county's beef cattle, the second largest herd among the state's counties, further contributed to Callaway's economic stability. While tobacco remained the county's most important nonfood cash crop, a few farmers raised small quantities of flax and hemp.[17]

Fulton, the seat of Callaway County and its largest town, enjoyed the benefits of the agricultural productivity of the surrounding countryside. The community experienced rapid growth in its first decade, and by 1840 boasted a variety of merchants and artisans who maintained thriving businesses, in addition to several small-scale manufacturing firms that produced for the local market, among them two carriage shops, two wagon factories, a tannery, and a wool-carding mill. By the early 1850s, the town had become a major regional market and had developed regular means of transportation to and communication with other Missouri towns and cities. Its trade had fostered the development of ten mercantile houses and three hotels, and Fulton served as the main depot for several stagecoach routes, all operated by a company that maintained in the town stables and a wagon and blacksmith's shop at which repairs were made on the firm's coaches.[18]

By the mid 1850s Fulton had also begun to develop a number of institutions that lent some prestige to the young community, in addition to the county courthouse, the center of local government and politics. In 1850, the Rev. William W. Robertson, pastor of the Fulton Presbyterian Church and a man filled with the educational zeal typical of ministers of his denomination, founded the Fulton Female Seminary, the town's first institution of higher learning. A year later the Reverend Robertson was instrumental in the founding of Fulton College, which in 1853 became Westminster College. By the end of the 1840s, Fulton and Callaway County had also attracted the attention of the state legislature, and in 1847 that

12

body chartered the State Lunatic Asylum, to be built in Fulton. That institution opened its doors in 1851, as did the Missouri School for the Deaf, which the legislature had also placed in Fulton.[19]

In 1855 a Fulton resident writing to the *Missouri Republican*, a St. Louis newspaper, boasted of his town's seminary and college, the State Lunatic Asylum, the State School for the Deaf, the town's five churches, its twenty stores, and its growing legal community attracted to Fulton by the county courthouse. Fulton, a town of 1,200, despite its youth was a place where, the correspondent continued, "an elevated tone of morals pervades the community." It was a town "located in rich farming country, peopled with some of the choicest society (numbering among it many old Kentucky and some Virginia families) blessed with literary institutions of a high order and the great charities of the state, and the scene of scarcely any intemperance." If this correspondent's vision of the community was typical of that held by most residents, then in the mid-1850s we infer that the people of Fulton were extremely pleased with and proud of their accomplishments.[20]

Among those citizens benefiting from, and contributing to, the growth of Fulton was John Jameson, who arrived in the recently created town in 1825 from Montgomery County, Kentucky. A man in his early twenties with a common school education obtained in his native state, Jameson first sought to earn a livelihood as a miller. He built a mill, probably a combination grist and sawmill, soon after his arrival. A personable fellow, Jameson quickly earned the trust and respect of his fellow townspeople. In the summer of 1825 he was selected to a committee to plan a "grand barbecue and celebration of the 4th of July." At this celebration, attended by some four hundred men and women, the young Jameson delivered his first address, performed well, and "was warmly congratulated by his friends on his first and successful effort before a promiscuous body." Whether because this venture instilled in him the desire for a political career or because his mill proved economically unsatisfactory, Jameson began to read law in the same year under one of Fulton's first attorneys, William Lucas. He completed his studies of the law the following year, was admitted to the Missouri bar, and immediately opened his own practice. With his practice which was successful from the start, he managed to support himself, his wife Susan, and a growing family that would eventually include four children—one boy and three girls. By 1830 his practice was secure enough to allow Jameson to venture into politics, and he stood for and was elected to a seat in the Missouri General Assembly on the Democratic ticket. His election launched a successful political career, which in turn enhanced his reputation as one of Fulton's leading attorneys.[21]

Just as Robert Newsom had amassed a sizable estate in rural Callaway County by the mid-1850s, John Jameson had become one of Fulton's more prosperous residents. By 1850 his success at the bar had provided him the means to acquire real property valued at $3,200, almost precisely the value of Newsom's farm. And like Robert Newsom, Jameson had invested in human property. Unlike the farmer Newsom, however, Jameson had little need of an all-male labor force. Rather, as a professional, indeed, as a prominent public figure and family man residing in the town of Fulton, he required domestic servants to help attend to the running of a large household. Thus, the 1850 slave schedules show that Jameson owned four slaves, at least some of whom, if not all, would have been employed as domestics. The age and sex of the slaves suggest that Jameson probably owned two couples, a pair composed of a male age 48 and a female age 35, and a second pair containing a male age 22 and female age 16.[22]

Jameson had also become one of Fulton and Callaway County's most respected citizens. After his initial term in the General Assembly, Jameson was twice reelected, serving as speaker of the house from 1834 to 1836, and thus significantly increasing Fulton's influence within the legislature. In 1839 he was elected to fill a seat in the House of Representatives left vacant by the death of Congressman Albert Harrison. He chose not to run for reelection in 1840. Whether his decision was based on personal reasons or internal party politics is not known, but it established a rather curious pattern in Jameson's developing political career. His decision might also have been influenced by the fact that Congressional seats were contested on a general, statewide ticket, rather than by district. He successfully stood for reelection to the House in 1842 and served in the twenty-eighth Congress. In 1844 he once again declined a reelection bid, only to enter the congressional campaign in 1846 and reclaim his old seat for a final term, returning to Fulton and his law practice for good in the spring of 1849.[23]

Thus in 1855, Jameson, now 53, had a flourishing law practice, a pleasant home in Fulton, and what appeared to be the perfect family. Like Robert Newsom, he was not a wealthy man but enjoyed considerable financial security. No longer active in politics, he enjoyed additional time to devote to Susan, his wife; John H., his only son, age sixteen; and daughters Elizabeth, fourteen; Sarah, twelve; and Malinda, ten. Since his political retirement he had also developed a second professional interest, one which could only enhance his status in the community—the ministry. Jameson had become a divinity student, obtaining ordination as a minister in the Christian church. Like Robert Newsom, John Jameson seemed to be the ideal family man, a successful, respected citizen, and a pillar of the community.[24] Of the two men, however, only one was what he seemed.

Two

The Crime

Controversy over slavery was nothing new for Missouri. The very creation of the state launched a national debate about the institution, the country's first serious effort to probe the moral implications of slavery for a free and increasingly democratic society. At precisely the time that Robert Newsom was beginning his struggle to create a new life for his family in the Missouri wilderness, the nation was determining whether, and under what conditions, Missouri could be admitted to the Union. Since the conclusion of the War of 1812, several economic and social factors had contributed to an influx of settlers from the east, swelling Missouri's territorial population to the point that statehood seemed inevitable. However, Missouri's formal request for statehood in 1819 was to meet with unexpected resistance in Congress. For the first time since ratification of the Constitution, members of Congress seriously debated forcing a territory to abandon slavery as the price for admission into the Union.

These congressional debates over slavery in Missouri rocked

16

the nation. Representative James Tallmadge of New York had joined the issue with a resolution amending legislation to grant Missouri statehood by requiring that Missouri prohibit the further introduction of slavery and free all slave children born within the state upon their twenty-fifth birthday. The Tallmadge amendment touched off a furor in the halls of Congress, especially as northern Congressmen now began to question the morality of slavery. Southerners, among them Senator William Smith of South Carolina, responded by beginning to develop a positive defense of what was their own peculiar institution. For more than a year the debate raged, in state legislatures, in party caucuses, in the partisan newspapers, in the House and Senate. Thoughtful men, North and South, Jeffersonian Republican and Federalist alike, immediately sensed the gravity of the debates and feared for the future of the nation. An alarmed John Quincy Adams saw the debates as "a mere preamble—a title page to a great tragic volume." In the South, an aging Thomas Jefferson wrote that the Missouri controversy "like a fire bell in the night, awakened and filled me with terror. I considered it the death knell of the Union." Henry Clay, John C. Calhoun, Daniel Morril, William Hunter, and others searched anxiously for a workable compromise in this emotionally charged atmosphere of Congress.[1]

Missourians who had emigrated from southeastern slave states, bringing their human chattels with them, were appalled that congressional action threatened to deprive them of a form of property perfectly legal in half the states of the Union. The newspapers of the territory spoke with one voice: Congress should not place restrictions upon Missouri's right to enter the Union. Even some in Missouri, especially in the St. Louis area, who saw slavery as an evil that could be gradually eliminated, opposed congressional efforts to force Missouri to accept gradual abolition as a condition of gaining admission to the Union. Throughout 1819, Missourians condemned the

Tallmadge amendment at mass meetings, public dinners, and even at religious gatherings. Thomas Hart Benton increased his popularity with fiery denouncements of the restrictionists, and Missouri's citizens drank toasts urging the next Congress to welcome Tallmadge's supporters with "a dark room, a straight waistcoat and a thin water gruel diet." A few opponents of slavery in the St. Louis area braved prevailing sentiments, holding a public meeting to endorse the Tallmadge amendment, but most who held such sentiments kept them to themselves.[2]

In this national crisis the desire to preserve the Union proved stronger than the sectional differences over slavery, and a compromise was negotiated. In 1821 Missouri was admitted to the Union as a slave state, Maine as a free state, and slavery's expansion into the Louisiana Territory was limited to that area south of Missouri. In a controversy that had rehearsed practically every aspect of future debates over slavery, northern congressmen had bowed to the South's demands and therefore made compromise possible. Not only had the South gained additional territory for the expansion of slavery, it had also acquired federal recognition of the legitimacy of the institution. Perhaps more significantly, the compromise and the defeat of the Tallmadge amendment gave notice of the South's commitment to the permanence of slavery. Slavery, the compromise asserted, was not merely a necessary evil, an institution that could be eliminated within a generation or two, or whose fate could be determined by a congressional majority. Rather, slavery was an institution fundamental to the existence of southern society, a permanent part of the southern way of life.[3]

The people of Missouri, adamantly opposed to congressional efforts to force them to abolish slavery, cheered the passage of the compromise. It is very likely that Robert Newsom and his neighbors in Callaway County were among the celebrants. They may not have fully understood the significance of the Missouri debates, or the complex legal and political concepts advanced by the constitutional theorists on both sides, but they certainly would have understood that the compromise enabled them to pursue their dreams of economic prosperity—dreams that had been formulated in the slaveholding states of the southeast, dreams that included the acquiring of human chattels. And so, with Missouri safely in the Union and the immediate future of the institution of slavery assured, Robert Newsom and his fellow residents of Callaway County set out to act upon their dreams.

They were remarkably successful. The agricultural prosperity achieved by residents of Callaway County and by the Robert Newsom family, despite the fact that none of the southern cash crops were grown in large quantities, depended heavily on slave labor. Flourishing as a result of the hard work and driving ambition of its residents, Callaway quickly became one of the new state's leading slaveholding counties. By 1850 slaveholding was widespread, and slaves made up approximately 40 percent of the county's population. By the end of the next decade, Callaway ranked fourth among Missouri's counties in the number of slaves held. The actual pattern of slave ownership reflected the nature of an agricultural economy dominated by farmers, rather than planters, which was typical of Missouri, although the state had some large plantations. Although over half the county's white families in 1850 held slaves, relatively few individuals held large numbers of slaves. Of the county's 809 slaveowners in 1850, 706 held fewer than ten slaves; 489 owners, or more than half, held four slaves or less. Only 102 slaveowners held ten or more slaves. Although slaves were also engaged in a variety of nonagricultural tasks, and some were owned by individuals

19

in nonfarm occupations, the majority of Callaway's slaves were owned by farmers. Slaves frequently worked alongside their masters in the fields, from which they produced much of the county's rich agricultural harvest. Quite clearly, slave ownership was economically advantageous for the farmers of Callaway, for census data demonstrate that each adult slave owned increased the output of the family farm.[4]

Thus it is hardly surprising that Robert Newsom, like many of Callaway County's farmers, invested some of his newly acquired capital in human chattels. It was a logical investment, since a Callaway farmer could readily deduce from the experience of his neighbors that the purchase of slaves held the potential both to increase the production of his farm and to enhance his social standing within the community. By the time the census taker arrived at his farm in 1850, Newsom had acquired five slaves: four adult males and a five-year-old boy.[5] Sometime soon afterward, probably within the same year, Newsom would decide to purchase his sixth slave. It would prove a momentous decision.

Although slave ownership would definitely have tended to increase his social status, economic gain appears the motive for Newsom's slave purchases before 1850. Except for the five-year-old boy, all of the slaves Newsom held at the time of that year's census were unquestionably purchased to increase the farm's productivity. They were prime hands: young men ranging in age from eighteen to thirty-one years. The presence of the five-year-old boy is more difficult to explain. Young slave children usually resided with their mothers who were primarily responsible for their care. Neither adult male slaves nor white slaveowning families would have ordinarily been engaged in caring for a slave child of this age, although it is possible the child was the son of one of the male slaves. From Newsom's perspective, however, the child's potential value would have been offset by the cost of his care until his labor could be used productively, or until he could be sold for a price based upon his ability as a laborer. The ownership of so young a slave would not have contributed significantly to Newsom's social status.

Such was not the case with his next purchase, a teenage girl named Celia, whom Newsom purchased in neighboring Audrain County. How Newsom came to know she was for sale we do not know—perhaps through an ad in the *Fulton Telegraph*, perhaps from a flyer posted in Fulton or at a crossroads store, perhaps by word of mouth. What is certain is that Newsom's reasons for acquiring Celia were different from those that motivated his previous slave purchases. Newsom was not seeking a field hand or a domestic servant to aid his daughters with the drudgery of daily household operations. Rather, subsequent events reveal that he had set out to purchase a replacement for his wife, dead now for nearly a year.

Prosperity, some standing in the community, and the support of his children, who were now grown and living either with him or nearby, did not satisfy Newsom. Virginia, his oldest daughter, had probably assumed the duties of mistress of the house upon her mother's death, a task she very likely shared with her younger sister, Mary. However successful they were in assuming the responsibilities of running the Newsom household, Newsom still lacked a wife. A healthy sixty years of age, Newsom needed more than a hostess and manager of household affairs; he required a sexual partner. Newsom seems to have deliberately chosen to purchase a young slave girl to fulfill this role, a choice made the more convenient by the ability to present the girl as a domestic servant purchased for the benefit of his daughters. The population demographics of Callaway County indicate that Newsom should have been able to obtain a bride from among the white female residents. Although Callaway County's white population in

1850 included slightly more males than females, the differential was so slight that it seems unlikely a prosperous farmer and respected community member such as Newsom would have encountered difficulty in finding a second wife.[6] It would not have been unusual for Newsom to select a bride from a less affluent family, and neither would it have been unusual for the chosen woman's family to give their subsequent blessing to such a union. As to whether Newsom's reasons for failing to remarry were social, economic, or purely personal, we can only guess. What is known is that from the moment he purchased Celia, Newsom regarded her as both his property and his concubine.

In that same year, perhaps indeed at the very time that Robert Newsom set out on his trip to purchase Celia, the nation and the state of Missouri were once again embroiled in a bitter debate over slavery. Precisely as had been the case thirty years earlier, when Newsom was struggling to carve a farm from Callaway's virgin forests, the nation was bitterly divided over the issue of slavery in the territories. Northern congressmen again sought to prevent the spread of slavery into territories gained as a result of the Mexican War, and to assure the admission of California into the Union as a free state. Led by John C. Calhoun, southern radicals prepared to dissolve the Union rather than see slavery prohibited in the western territories, for which soldiers from the South, most of them volunteers, had fought and died. Throughout the spring and summer the debate would rage in the House and Senate, until Henry Clay, Daniel Webster, Stephen Douglas, Howell Cobb, and others could hammer out a compromise.

Once again the people of Missouri were caught up in a national debate over slavery. Although this time they were not at the center of the debate, Missouri and its people were more deeply divided over the issue than they had been thirty years earlier. In St. Louis especially, there was little interest in the further expansion of slavery, whereas representatives of the large slaveholding counties along the Missouri River strongly opposed any effort to restrain the spread of the institution. A bitter fight erupted within the ranks of the state's Democratic party, as proslavery David Atchinson opposed his fellow Senator Thomas Hart Benton. The grand old man of Missouri's Democratic party and an ardent supporter of Andrew Jackson throughout his career, Benton had fought all efforts to disrupt the Union. He was opposed to the further expansion of slavery into the western territories, but his staunch support of the Union made him receptive to compromise. The rift in Democratic ranks would cost Benton his senate seat, secure Atchinson's position as spokesman for the state's proslavery Democrats, and create a permanent division within the party.[7]

When Robert Newsom set out on his journey to Audrain County to purchase Celia, he was probably aware of the debate over the expansion of slavery into the Mexican cession then tearing asunder the state's Democratic party. Such an awareness was practically guaranteed by the attention focused on the issue by local newspapers, by practicing politicians, and by those members of the general public who enjoyed following a rousing political debate in which they had some stake. As a prosperous slaveholder in a predominantly agricultural county, it is also likely that he favored Atchinson's uncompromising proslavery position over that of Benton. It is unlikely, though, that Newsom saw the political debates over slavery in the territories as having any practical bearing on his plans to purchase a female slave. He probably made the trip by wagon, as he had to travel a relatively long distance. Audrain County bordered Callaway to the north, and, since Newsom lived in southern Callaway, the journey would have covered approximately forty miles and required at least a day's ride each way.

The reasons Celia's former owner decided to put her up for sale are unknown, as is the owner's identity. All that is certain is that sometime in 1850 Newsom purchased Celia, who was at the time approximately fourteen years of age. Perhaps she had been born and reared on the estate of her previous owner, perhaps she was torn from her family or from another community to which she had belonged. Of the details of Celia's life before she was purchased by Newsom, we know nothing. Whatever her circumstances, she might well have faced her transfer to a new master with fear and foreboding. If so, her worst fears were soon confirmed.

On his return to Callaway County, Newsom raped Celia, and by that act at once established and defined the nature of the relationship between the master and his newly acquired slave. The emotional response of the master and his slave to this violent act lie outside the methods of historical inquiry. Nevertheless, the historical record can be used to draw some reasonable conclusions. It is possible, even probable, that Newsom felt no remorse for his act. We know that his rape of Celia was no isolated incident, the act of a demented individual, an event which, had it been immediately discovered, would have raised a storm of moral outrage among white southerners, including the residents of Callaway County. Rather, recent historical scholarship has confirmed abolitionist charges that slave women were frequently abused by white men. One historian writing on the significance of rape by whites as a determinant of black female behavior has observed that "virtually every known nineteenth-century female slave narrative contains a reference to, at some juncture, the ever present threat and reality of rape." Others have shown not only that female slaves were frequently raped by masters, but that white southerners were aware that the sexual abuse of female slaves was widespread. Indeed, the practice of white male slaveholders using female slaves for their sexual gratification had its defenders, though the practice was never condoned by public opinion.[8] Thus while it is impossible to know the thoughts of Robert Newsom at the time he raped his newly purchased slave, it is entirely possible that he felt that his ownership of the young Celia entitled him to use her for his sexual pleasure. Whatever Newsom's thoughts about the matter, the sexual nature of the relationship between master and slave, once established, would never change.

Celia's probable emotional response to Newsom's attack upon her is suggested both by research carried out with modern victims of rape and by recent historical scholarship. The historical record indicates that this was very likely Celia's initial sexual experience. For a number of reasons, including the slaves' own standards of morality, sexual activity among female slaves under fifteen years of age was uncommon.[9] Regardless of her previous sexual experience, however, Celia's rape by her new master would have been a psychologically devastating experience, one which would have had a profound effect upon her. Modern research indicates that rape victims experience a variety of responses: fear, rage, an overpowering sense of violation, sometimes helplessness, and a loss of self-esteem. The evidence suggests that while the victim's response is determined by her unique circumstances, most victims go through several stages before coming to terms with the fact of the rape and restructuring their lives.[10] Celia, however, had no opportunity to come to terms with a single incidence of rape, or to restructure her life. Life for Celia would entail continual sexual exploitation by her master.

The introduction of Celia into the Newsom household and the nature of her relationship to Robert, which continued throughout the five years she remained on the farm and would have been difficult to conceal, must have provoked reactions from other members of the family. It is possible that Newsom managed to conceal his relationship with Celia from the family. Or, family members might have chosen to ignore the relationship, to convince themselves that it did not exist. However, given the physical immediacy of life on a farm and the long-term nature of the relationship, neither of these possibilities is very likely. Virginia presumably experienced strong reactions to Celia's presence, as did the younger, unmarried Mary. Unfortunately, there exists no record of their reaction to the intrusion of this young woman into their father's household, or to her obvious role as his sexual partner. Recent scholarship, however, indicates that the response of Newsom's daughters to Celia was probably expressed in one of two forms. Anger and resentment was a characteristic response of white women in slaveholding households when faced with the possibility of a relationship between a male in the household and a female slave. Frequently, however, southern white women were powerless to prevent the actions of male family members, a circumstance that sometimes led them to vent their anger at white males upon the slave. Certainly neither Mary nor Virginia was in a position to change her father's conduct toward his slave, even had she so desired. Mary was still an adolescent herself, totally dependent upon her father, and Virginia had three children of her own to consider. She had little choice but to remain on her father's farm, regardless of her feelings about his behavior. On the other hand, the daughters may have seen their father as victim, Celia's unwitting conquest, since many southerners viewed black women as naturally sensual and promiscuous. Understandably, this view was more frequently expressed by white males, though it was also held by at least some white females and black males.[11]

The reaction of Newsom's sons toward Celia may have been quite different from that of their sisters. David, at seventeen, may have welcomed the presence of a female slave his age. It is possible even that he might have hoped to share her sexual favors. Recent scholarship has shown that there sometimes existed a willingness on the part of fathers and sons to share slave mistresses. Indeed, at approximately the time Celia was brought to Newsom's farm a much more famous southerner, Senator James Henry Hammond of South Carolina, was engaging in sexual relationships with two slave women, mother and daughter. He later gave both women to his legitimate son, Harry, who was also apparently involved in an affair with the daughter and who had fathered a child by her, as the elder Hammond admitted he may also have done.[12]

Thirty-seven and engaged to the woman who would become his second wife, Robert Newsom's oldest son, Harry, may or may not have objected to his father's actions. His response to Celia would have been influenced by the opinions of his betrothed (depending on the degree of his devotion to her), his attitudes about slavery, and the nature of his relationship to his father, both filial and economic. Whatever his feelings about his father's relationship to Celia, he would soon leave his father's farm to establish his own household. For this reason, and because of likely financial ties to his father or to his estate, it is doubtful that Harry would have chastised his father, even if he disapproved of his actions. Thus, regardless of what his children and grandchildren thought about his sexual abuse of the recently purchased young female slave, Robert Newsom was lord of the manor and could use Celia as he pleased.

Celia's arrival at the Newsom farm also would have required an adjustment by individuals other than family members. By this time, as we have seen, Robert Newsom had five male slaves, four of whom were older than Celia. As to their response to a new female slave on the farm, especially one obviously serving as concubine for their master, we can only surmise. Recent studies of the sexual behavior of slaves, however, indicate that despite the intrusion of the institution of slavery into their private lives, slaves accepted essentially the same conventions of sexual behavior that were prevalent among whites. Thus, although the census data do not indicate the presence of female slaves at the Newsom farm, some of Newsom's adult male slaves may well have had mates on surrounding farms, or in the town of Fulton, since such arrangements were common throughout the South.[13] Given human nature, however, there was also a high probability, one supported by recent scholarship on slavery, that one or more of the adult male slaves would have seen Celia as a possible sexual partner, a circumstance that would have created tensions between the slave and master.[14]

We know little about the dynamics of the human relationships on the Newsom farm between 1850 and 1855. Most of what we know must be gleaned from the records of her trial, but what is known indicates that Celia proved a troubling presence. Her assigned task on the farm seems to have been that of cook, but the testimony at her trial suggests that throughout the period Robert Newsom regarded her primarily as his concubine. He continued to make sexual demands of her, and Celia gave birth to two children, one, probably both, fathered by him. The evidence also indicates that, because of her special relationship to him, Newsom rewarded Celia with material goods beyond those which could ordinarily be expected by a slave. Certainly one such reward, at least from Newsom's point of view, if not from Celia's, was a cabin of her own, one that would have been luxurious compared to the housing in which the vast majority of American slaves resided. Built of brick, it was a one-story structure with a single front entrance and windows on the back. The cabin possessed a large chimney and fireplace complete with hearth stones, and was situated in a grove of cherry and pear trees some fifty yards behind the Newsom home.[15]

At some time before 1855, Celia became romantically involved with another of Newsom's slaves, a man named George. Little is known of the relationship, although Celia's trial record suggests that it developed toward the end of her stay on the Newsom farm. It must have been an intense relationship, for by early 1855 George had begun "staying" with Celia in her cabin. Whether his stays were for more than a night, and whether they were known to Newsom, we can only conjecture. What is known is that during this period Newsom continued to visit Celia regularly in her cabin and to have sexual intercourse with her. The very existence of this triangle suggests that Celia's relationship to George had only recently begun, for it is extremely unlikely that such a triangular relationship could have long endured without Newsom's knowledge. That Newsom had separated Celia from the male slaves on the farm and placed her in a special cabin close to his home strongly suggests that he was not prepared to tolerate her involvement with the male slaves. So, too, does George's insistence that Celia break off her relationship with Newsom.[16]

Sometime in the winter of 1855, probably in late February or early March, an event occurred that changed forever the human relationships on the Newsom farm. Celia again conceived, this time without certain knowledge of the father, knowing only that the child she carried had been sired either by her master, Robert Newsom, or by her fellow bondsman, George. Testimony given at Celia's trial suggests that Celia's pregnancy had placed an emotional strain upon George that he could not accept. Celia was his lover—he perhaps regarded her as his wife—yet he could not protect her from the sexual advances of the man who owned them both. At this time George faced a dilemma imposed by his own sense of masculinity and his inability to alter the behavior of his master. It was a dilemma common among male slaves, one that scholars agree was extremely detrimental to their status within the slave community and family. To have confronted Newsom directly at this stage to demand that he cease his sexual exploitation of Celia would have been an act that could have cost him his life. While some black males possessed the courage to take such risks, most, understandably, were unprepared to do so.[17] So George made a demand of the most vulnerable member of the triangle. According to testimony at Celia's trial, George informed Celia that "he would have nothing more to do with her if she did not quit the old man." The question of how she was to accomplish this, given the nature of her relationship to Newsom, George apparently left unanswered.[18]

George's ultimatum placed Celia in a quandary that exemplified perfectly the vulnerability of female slaves to sexual exploitation by males within the owner's household. Faced with sexual exploitation by a white male, especially an owner, a female slave had few options but to submit. Of course, physical resistance was possible, and slave women in similar circumstances did on occasion resort to physical attacks upon the males who threatened them, some resorting to murder. Such resistance, however, always carried the possibility of physical retaliation, perhaps even death. If a slave woman had children, as Celia did, physical resistance could also lead to retribution against her children, including their sale. Understandably, under such circumstances only the most determined, indomitable female slaves resisted their white exploiters physically. On large plantations, or in towns, a female slave might seek the protection of an individual whose power the master could not ignore—a white townsman of some prominence opposed to the sexual exploitation of slaves, for example. On larger plantations, the interceding individual could even be black, perhaps a black woman who had some standing within the plantation slave community. Celia, however, like many slaves, lacked the support of an organized slave community. She might have considered fleeing, one of the most prevalent forms of resistance among slaves, on plantations or on family farms, whether urban or rural. Here, again, she was handicapped by the presence of her children. In addition, there is no evidence to suggest that Celia had any contacts with the world beyond the Newsom farm, any relationships with persons, slave or free, who might aid her in an escape attempt. Finally, George's ultimatum clearly indicated that he would take no action to protect Celia from the advances of her master. The lone female slave on a family farm, lacking the support of a large slave community, cut off from the possible allies that might have been found in an urban setting, burdened with the responsibility for her two children, and unable to depend upon the protection of her slave lover, Celia was forced to confront her dilemma alone.[19]

Under such circumstances, it is a measure of her commitment to George that Celia attempted to do as he bid her, and to do so in a manner that held the possibility of allowing their relationship to continue. Any action she might have considered would have placed her in jeopardy. Actually confronting Newsom would have placed her person at risk and threatened the well-being of her children and the child she carried. To make an appeal to other adult members of the family also carried its dangers, since none of the family members were likely to have welcomed her open admission of Newsom's continued sexual exploitation of her. The latter course, however, carried the lesser risk, and was the one Celia selected. In an effort to stop Newsom's sexual advances and thus retain George's affections, she appealed to the family members, citing her pregnancy and accompanying sickness rather than her relationship with George. It is almost certain that Celia approached Virginia and Mary. She would have appealed first to them because they were women but also because by this time neither of the Newsom sons lived at their father's home. Harry had long had his own residence, and in April David and his new bride had moved to their own farm.[20]

The reaction of Newsom's daughters to Celia's revelations is unrecorded. Whether or not they believed her, we can never know, but it is difficult to imagine that they were not already painfully aware of the nature of the relationship between Celia and their father. Nor does the evidence indicate whether either Virginia or Mary attempted to intervene with their father on Celia's behalf. It is extremely unlikely that either did so, for they were nearly as dependent upon their father as was Celia. Mary, at approximately nineteen yet a youth herself, could have done nothing to prevent her father's abuse of Celia. Virginia, a thirty-six-year-old mother of three children who, for whatever reason, was without husband, was dependent upon her father for both her own well-being and for that of her children. Economic dependence upon their father, however, is not the only factor that would have made intervention by the daughters on Celia's behalf unlikely. Women within the South's slaveholding families were, after all, beneficiaries of slavery, and as such unlikely critics. In addition, the society furnished them a variety of rationalizations, just as it offered a number of justifications for the dominant role of the male. While slavery had its white female southern critics, white women were on the whole supportive of the institution, in addition to being relatively powerless to prevent the sexual exploitation of female slaves, which they bitterly resented.[21]

What is certain is that at this point in their lives, both of Newsom's daughters experienced what Charles Sellers has called "the fundamental moral anxiety" of slavery. They were forced to confront one of slavery's oldest and most painful moral dilemmas. To do nothing meant that Celia would continue to be sexually exploited by their father. To confront their father would possibly threaten their own livelihood and continued well-being and, in Virginia's case, the well-being of her children. Their dilemma was made the more acute by Celia's threat to hurt the old man "if he did not quit forcing her while she was sick." Perhaps they escaped their dilemma through a process of rationalization, as a historian of slavery recently has suggested many plantation women did, viewing Celia as the dark, sensual temptress who seduced their father. Perhaps they accepted the power of the patriarch, as their society bid them do, viewing an obedient acceptance of their father's behavior as an obligation. Whatever they thought about Celia and her relationship with their father as a result of Celia's appeal, there is no evidence to indicate that either daughter acted to prevent her abuse by their father.[22]

Whether or not Virginia and Mary attempted to intervene on Celia's behalf, Newsom's behavior did not change. He continued to make sexual demands of Celia. Driven by Newsom's unceasing sexual advances and George's demand that she force Newsom to stop having sexual relations with her, Celia directly confronted her master sometime on or immediately before June 23, 1855. Faced with rejection by her lover, she begged Newsom to leave her alone, again using the excuse that as a result of her pregnancy she had been sick for the last few months rather than revealing the nature of her relationship with George.

Newsom's response to Celia's plea was predictable. Whatever he thought of or felt for her, whether he regarded her as a person or experienced even an occasional stirring of compassion for her, we cannot know. It is possible that he felt all of these things, or none. His past behavior toward Celia, however, unequivocally proclaimed that, whatever he felt for Celia, as her master he considered sexual relations with her his privilege. Thus Newsom brushed aside her request and, as if to emphasize his right to sex with her, informed Celia that "he was coming to her cabin that night."[23]

33

Desperately seeking some means of complying with George's ultimatum, Celia threatened to hurt her master if he made further sexual demands of her. Newsom's response to Celia's threats is not recorded, but nothing in any of the testimony given at Celia's trial indicates that he took seriously threats from a slave girl who had served as his mistress for almost five years. Celia, on the other hand, was determined to break off the sexual relationship with her master, even if it meant acting upon her threats. After her confrontation with Newsom, Celia obtained a large stick, which she placed in the corner of her cabin upon her return. Should Newsom come to her cabin that night, as he said he would, Celia was prepared to resort to a physical attack to repel his advances.[24]

As evening approached on Saturday, June 23, the members of the Newsom family prepared for bed. Since David and his bride had moved to their own home in April, only Mary, Virginia, and Virginia's children remained in the household with Newsom. Virginia last saw her father at twilight, sitting by his bedroom window reading. She had probably entered the bedroom to place her youngest son, Billy, who slept with his grandfather, in bed. Then Mary, Virginia, and the other children, including James Coffee, who slept in the room with his mother, retired for the night, leaving Newsom alone with his book and young Billy. It was the last time any member of the family saw him.[25]

Later that night, at approximately ten o'clock, after the other family members were asleep, Newsom left his bedroom and walked the sixty or so paces to Celia's cabin. He entered the cabin, which was illuminated by the light from a small fire Celia had started in the fireplace. We know that Celia's children were in the cabin with her, but because of the late hour it is likely they were asleep. Precisely what occurred in the few minutes after Newsom entered the cabin is unclear. It is reasonable to assume that Newsom, as was his custom, went to the cabin solely for the purpose of having sexual intercourse with Celia. Since Celia had warned her master not to come to her cabin again for that purpose, and had threatened to hurt him if he did so, it is also reasonable to assume that a confrontation occurred. We do know from testimony at Celia's trial that the two exchanged words. Whatever else was said, we know that Newsom demanded that Celia continue to have sex with him and that Celia refused.

As Newsom approached her, Celia retreated before him into a corner of the house, with Newsom positioned between her and the fireplace, his form silhouetted against the flames. Celia reached into the corner and retrieved the large stick that she had placed there earlier in the afternoon precisely for the purpose of defending herself should Newsom ignore her warnings. As the old man continued to advance, with one hand she raised the stick, "about as large as the upper part of a Windsor chair, but not so long," and brought it down against the head of her master. Dazed by the blow, Newsom "sunk down on a stool or towards the floor," groaning and throwing up his hands as if to catch Celia. Afraid that an angered Newsom would harm her, Celia raised the club with both hands and once again brought it crashing down on Newsom's skull. With the second blow the old man fell, dead, to the floor.[26]

Frightened by what she had done, Celia for a moment could only stare at the prone figure of her master. Then she bent down to examine him, "to see whether he was dead." Her examination revealed that she had killed Newsom, and momentarily she panicked. She realized her danger, feared that Newsom's body would be discovered and she would be hung. She had to think, to regain her composure. With Newsom's corpse sprawled upon her floor, it was imperative that she discover a method of disposing of the body, one which would draw no suspicion toward her, which would not reveal that Newsom had visited her cabin. She sat for an hour or more, watching the still figure on her cabin floor, perhaps checking to see that her children, after all the commotion, were still sleeping.

Finally she hit upon a plan, one both simple and ironic. She decided to burn Newsom's body in her fireplace. With his body consumed by flames, there would be nothing left to connect her with her master's disappearance, nothing to indicate that he had come to her that night. Celia took the stick with which she had killed Newsom and laid it in the fire. She stepped outside and collected staves intended for hogsheads, which were stacked near the cabin. Returning, she built a roaring fire, then doubled up the body of Newsom and pushed it into the flames. Through the night she tended the fire as it consumed the mortal remains of her former master. When the flames had disposed of the body, she picked the remaining bones from the ashes, crushing the smaller ones against the hearth stones with a rock and throwing the crushed particles back into the fireplace. The larger bones, those she could not crush, she placed "under the hearth, and under the floor between a sleeper and the fire-place." When the ashes cooled, she worked in the dark to remove some of the ashes, which she carried out into the yard just before daybreak. Then she went to bed.[27]

The next morning, before the family became alarmed at the absence of Robert Newsom, Celia spied the twelve-year-old Coffee Waynescot playing in a cherry tree outside her cabin. In an act that revealed the depth of her hatred for Newsom and his kin, she asked the boy to come into her cabin and clean out her fireplace. Coffee testified that "she would give me two dozen walnuts if I would carry the ashes out. I said good lick." And so, enticed by a slave's offer of a handful of walnuts, Coffee Waynescot climbed down from the cherry tree and entered Celia's cabin. Accompanied by Celia he walked over to the hearth on which Celia cooked her family's meals. There he bent down and scooped the ashes from the fireplace, dropping them from his ash shovel into a bucket. As the shovelfuls of ash thudded against the bucket bottom, ash particles would have arisen from the bucket and floated and swirled in the morning air. Stooped over the hearth within the confines of Celia's small cabin, Coffee Waynescot inevitably would have inhaled the remains of his grandfather, would have breathed his grandfather's ashes deep into his lungs. What Celia, a slave, felt at that moment is not recorded, but she would have understood that the boy was inhaling his grandfather's remains even as he cleared the ashes from the fireplace, a fireplace which Coffee's grandfather had built for her, and over which she cooked the food she fed her own children, whom Robert Newsom had fathered. The ashes removed from the fireplace, young Coffee carried the bucket outside and spilled his grandfather's remains in the grass alongside a "beat down like" path which ran to the stables that had only the day before belonged to Robert Newsom.[28]

Three

Inquisition

Sometime early in the morning of Sunday, June 24, 1855, Virginia and Mary Newsom became concerned about their father, who had not appeared for the morning meal. Their increasing concern about their father's disappearance, a fear that something was amiss, prompted the daughters to begin to search for him. Virginia looked first along "all the paths and walks and every place for him" without success. Next she searched along the creek, fearing that Newsom had fallen into the creek and drowned. The women hunted for Robert Newsom in the coves along the creek banks, but "found no trace of him." At this point the daughters, evidently realizing that their efforts alone were unlikely to locate their father, called upon their neighbors for help. By ten o'clock that morning William Powell, whose farm adjoined the Newsom place, had joined with other neighbors to help Virginia and Mary look for their father. Someone carried the news of his father's disappearance to Harry Newsom, who immediately went to join the search. When he arrived at his father's home sometime before noon, Harry found others, including Powell, already engaged in the hunt for his father. The search continued in vain until someone, probably a member of the Newsom family, suggested that George, Celia's lover, might be able to provide some information. That George was singled out strongly suggests that family members were aware of the nature of his relationship with Celia and suspected that jealousy might have caused him to harm Newsom.[1]

The search party located George and brought him forward for questioning. William Powell, who seems to have assumed leadership of the search party despite the presence of Harry Newsom, conducted George's interrogation. Powell's keen interest in the fate of Newsom was very likely prompted by more than the fact that they were neighbors. The almost uncanny similarities in their lives provided Powell reasons aplenty to take a personal interest in Newsom's disappearance. Like Newsom, Powell had migrated westward to Missouri seeking cheap, fertile land on which to raise a family and seek his fortune. Born in Maryland in 1814, he had moved with his family to Kentucky three years later, where he was raised on a farm and educated in common schools. In 1836 he married Sallie Bowles and moved to Missouri, settling in Callaway County alongside the already prospering farm of Robert Newsom. Powell, too, had suffered the loss of a wife. In fact, he had lost two wives; he lost his first wife in childbirth a year after their marriage, and in 1839 married Jane Cheatham, by whom he had four more children. Jane also died in childbirth in 1846, and within the year Powell had remarried. He chose Mary Fitzhugh as wife and mother to his children, and the couple would have seven more offspring. Powell's financial fortunes, like those of Robert Newsom, had prospered, and by 1850 he owned some 160 acres of land valued at $800, most of which was cleared and productive.

Like Newsom, Powell was also a slaveowner, in 1850 of a male slave aged 36 and a female slave 16. Thus if Powell retained the slaves he held in 1850, he would have been the owner, in 1855, of at least one adult male slave and a female slave approximately two years older than Celia. As the owner of a female slave Celia's age, who most likely had contact with Celia (although there is no record that she did so), Powell could hardly have been an objective inquisitor.[2]

George, who no doubt by this time understood the seriousness of the situation, was a reluctant witness when confronted by Powell. He certainly had every reason to be frightened by the accusations of an angry delegation of whites. He may also have wanted to protect Celia. This explanation, of course, assumes that Celia had informed George of Newsom's fate, a circumstance that was entirely possible, even probable, given their relationship, though nothing in Celia's trial record indicates that she had. Powell first asked George, whom he described as Newsom's "Negro boy," where he thought Newsom was. George replied that he did not know, but believed "it was not worth while to hunt for him any where except close around the house." This response led Powell to conclude that George knew more than he was telling, and Powell informed George that "he had better go and show us the old man if he knew where he was." This admonition from Powell strongly suggests he believed that George knew Newsom's whereabouts, or what had become of him, and that George was threatened with bodily harm, or worse, if he did not immediately reveal all that he knew about Newsom's disappearance.[3]

George now confronted his own moral dilemma, for it was he who had forced Celia to confront her master. It was George's ultimatum that if Celia wished to continue her relationship with him she would somehow have to end her sexual involvement with Newsom. And since George had felt it necessary to deliver that ultimatum, it seems reasonable to assume that Celia, for a variety of understandable reasons, including her concern for her children, had not been inclined to confront her master. While it is possible that Celia may have taken action against Newsom of her own accord, the evidence strongly suggests that she confronted Newsom only when forced to do so if she wished to continue her relationship with George. Although there is no evidence to link George directly to Newsom's death, it is very likely that he knew of Celia's threats to harm Newsom if he insisted on continuing to sleep with her. It is quite possible, indeed likely, that George knew that Celia had made such threats to both Newsom and his daughters. Given the size of the Newsom farm and the time that had lapsed between Newsom's death and George's confrontation with the search party, George very well may have been in contact with Celia that morning, and thus learned of Newsom's gruesome fate. Even if George had been unaware of Celia's threats against Newsom and of Newsom's death, he would have known that Celia would come under suspicion because of the nature of her relationship to Newsom, a relationship of which he was all too aware.

Whatever the exact nature of Powell's threat, George undoubtedly feared for his own life and chose to sacrifice Celia rather than to protect her. George's response indicated that he was aware that Newsom was no longer alive and that Celia was somehow involved with his fate. He informed Powell that "he believed the last walking [Newsom] had done was along the path, pointing to the path leading from the house to the Negro Cabin." While this response could have been conjecture, the few specifics contained, especially the specific reference to Celia's cabin, strongly suggest George had some knowledge of the events of the preceding night. Such knowledge could only have come from Celia, unless one assumes that George either participated in Newsom's murder or had been outside Celia's cabin, close enough to overhear the murder. Whatever the source of George's knowledge, Powell, from this and other statements George made, concluded that Newsom "had been destroyed in the Negro Cabin."[4] How this revelation affected Powell we do not know, but if he was still the master of a young slave woman, George's suggestions that Newsom had come to harm in Celia's cabin must have caused him considerable personal concern.

Alarmed by the information George had supplied, Powell and the others, including Harry Newsom, proceeded immediately to Celia's cabin, where they expected to find the corpse of a murdered Robert Newsom. They searched the premises but found nothing. It never occurred to them to examine the ashes remaining in the cabin's fireplace. Had they done so, the mystery of Newsom's disappearance would have been solved and their suspicions amply confirmed. Finding nothing in the cabin, Powell and his followers then sought to question Celia. Whether because of her children, because of her illness and pregnancy, because of her love and concern for George, or because she believed she had so efficiently and thoroughly disposed of Newsom's body that his disappearance could not be connected to her, Celia had made no effort to flee. She was easily located going about her normal duties in the kitchen of the Newsom home and brought before Powell's tribunal of Newsom family and friends.[5]

Convinced by his questioning of George that Celia knew what had happened to Newsom and suspecting the worst, Powell wasted no time in his confrontation with Celia. He was determined to use any means necessary to obtain information from her. Powell began his inquisition with accusations rather than questions. He bluntly told her that she knew what had become of Newsom and that members of the search party knew that she knew. An obvious untruth, Powell's assertion was designed to forestall any attempt by Celia to be less than forthcoming. He also deliberately sought to break Celia's will to resist by breaking her emotionally. Thus he prefaced his interrogation by informing her that George had told the search party enough to make them believe that "she knew where her master was."

If Powell expected an immediate confession from Celia he was disappointed. He had some reason to expect Celia to break easily, to feel that she would be unable to withstand his questioning. She faced the family members, friends, and neighbors of the master she had killed. She knew that members of Newsom's family were aware that she had threatened him. She certainly would have feared for her own life and thus for the fate that would befall her children. The news of George's cooperation with Powell and the Newsom family must have come as a shock to Celia, even if she understood the reasons for it. Under such circumstances she could hardly avoid feeling utterly alone, abandoned by the man she loved, whose demands had placed her in this position. George's desertion would have been an especially devastating emotional blow if, as his responses to Powell indicate was entirely possible, she had that morning informed George about what had become of Newsom. Under these circumstances she would have had to take seriously Powell's statement that the search party did, indeed, know of Newsom's demise, and that George had told the search party all that he knew.

Celia's initial response to Powell's questions was a defiant denial of any knowledge of Newsom's activities or his whereabouts. Her adamant denial argues against the possibility that she had provided George a detailed account of what had become of Newsom, although it does not eliminate it. Indeed, if Celia believed she had so efficiently disposed of Newsom's body that his death could never be confirmed, her denial can be seen as a way of protecting both herself and George. Whether or not she had told George of the

events of the preceding night, her flat denial of any knowledge of Newsom's fate indicates both an incredible bravery
and self-confidence. This initial denial indicates that Celia
believed, or hoped, that the search party would be unable
to locate Newsom's remains, and that she could deceive her
inquisitors. It also strongly implies that Celia suffered no pangs
of contrition.

Angered by Celia's staunch denials, Powell began to make
threats. First he directed an unspecified threat at Celia, telling
her that things would go better for her if she would tell the
truth. Unmoved by these general threats against herself, Celia
continued to deny Powell's charges, insisting that she had no
knowledge of what had become of Newsom. Powell then
changed his strategy, appealing to Celia's love for her children.
He told her that "her children should not be taken away from
her if she would tell." This approach held no real threat for
Celia, since her children certainly would have been taken from
her as soon as she revealed any knowledge of Newsom's fate.
Not surprisingly, Celia again refused to confess, adamantly
denying that she knew anything of Newsom's disappearance.
Powell then threatened her life, telling Celia that he "had a
rope provided for her if she did not tell." Despite these threats,
Celia continued to refuse to admit any guilt and steadfastly
maintained that she had no knowledge of Newsom's activities
or of his whereabouts.

Convinced that she was lying, Powell pressed forward with
his questioning, undoubtedly continuing to threaten the lives
of Celia and her children. For a period of considerable, though
unspecified, length, Celia retained her composure, ignored
the threats, and remained adamant in her refusal to respond.
Gradually, however, Powell's insistent questioning and continued threats broke Celia's resistance. Finally, she admitted
that Newsom had come to her cabin the preceding night.
Newsom, she said, had come to the window at the back of

44

the cabin, insisting that she have sex with him. Celia told
Powell that Newsom had not entered her cabin, however.
Rather, she said she struck Newsom as he leaned inside the
window. Still, Celia refused to admit to her inquisitors that she
was responsible for Newsom's disappearance, and continued
to deny that she knew what had become of him. After she
struck him, Celia continued, "he fell back on the outside and
she saw nothing more of him."

Celia's partial confession failed to satisfy Powell, since it
neither explained Newsom's disappearance nor helped to locate him. Yet her admission that she had seen Newsom the
previous night, and that she had struck him, gave Powell
an advantage. Powell resumed his interrogation, but, having acknowledged her confrontation with Newsom, Celia
"refused for sometime to tell anything more." Alone with
her captors, knowing that she had been abandoned by George,
and under the pressure of constant threats to herself and her
children, Celia finally could no longer resist. Evidence also
indicates that Celia had remained so adamant in her refusal
to confess because she feared that if she told Powell what had
happened, she would be killed on the spot by members of the
Newsom family. Celia's inquisitors were merely a collection
of family members, neighbors, and friends. The group had
no legal standing, and no representative of the law or the
court system was present. Although it is doubtful that Celia
would have known her rights under Missouri law, she certainly would have understood that confessing to Newsom's
murder, especially to the details of disposing of his body, in
the presence of two of his adult sons would place her life in
immediate danger. Celia promised to reveal what she knew
about Newsom upon the condition that Powell "send the two
men out of the room." The two men, although not identified
in Powell's testimony, were undoubtedly Harry and David
Newsom, both of whom had arrived by this time to help

search for their father. Powell convinced the two to leave, and Celia proceeded to give him a detailed confession as she had promised.[6]

The manner in which Powell responded to Celia's gruesome revelation can only be imagined, but her confession was certain to have impressed upon him the dangers of holding human beings in bondage. If he was himself the master of a young slave girl, and even if Powell treated his slaves decidedly better than did Newsom, Celia's confession must have at least caused Powell to consider how his female slave regarded him. Whatever his thoughts about the personal significance of the confession his threats had forced from Celia, Powell continued to maintain control of the situation. He promptly summoned the others, including David, Harry, and Mary Newsom and Virginia and Coffee Waynescot, and began a search for Newsom's remains to confirm Celia's story. Confirmation was quickly obtained. The search party, accompanied by George, located Newsom's ashes where Celia had said Coffee Waynescot had placed them, along the pathway leading past her cabin to the stables.

Their worst fears now confirmed, members of the search party began the gruesome task of extracting from the ashes the bits and pieces of Newsom's bones the flames had failed to consume. As the bone fragments were found, several members of the party, including Virginia, placed them in the hands of Harry Newsom, who wrapped his father's bones in paper and stored them in a box for safekeeping. Virginia found her father's gallus buckle in the ashes, along with "buttons my sister [Mary] sewed on my fathers' breeches a few days before his death." George discovered and turned over to the white members of the search party Newsom's pocketknife, its handle burned black by the flames.[7]

After the party had sifted through the ashes found beside the pathway, Virginia Waynescot and others once again entered

Celia's cabin to retrieve the bones that Celia had said she
hid beneath the hearth. Virginia turned over a large hearth
stone and discovered yet more of her father's bones. She also
met a yet more gruesome discovery. In searching for bones
she noticed that "the ashes were caked up in the fireplace."
She broke open the lumps of ash, which "looked as if something had been burned in them." Once broken, the lumps
of ash emitted a "strange smell." What remained of Robert
Newsom, which formed the lumps of ash Virginia Waynescot
held in her hands, fortunately looked "nothing like flesh." In
a remarkable display of composure under such circumstances,
Virginia Newsom calmly replaced the clumps of ash that had
been her father's flesh in the fireplace. She then placed the
bones of her father retrieved from the hearth in the box of
bones her brother had given her. She took the box filled with
Newsom's remains to her room, where she kept it upon her
bureau until an inquest into her father's death could be held.
Into another box she put the personal items found by the
search party: her father's gallus buckle, his buttons, and his
knife. This box, too, she kept in her room until the authorities
arrived.[8]

On the following morning, Monday, June 25, the official
case of the *State of Missouri versus Celia, a Slave* began. Because
all of the individuals involved in the official proceedings were
on hand early on the morning of June 25, it is evident that
preparations for an inquest had been made sometime during
the evening of Sunday, June 24. Two justices of the peace
from neighboring Cedar Township, D. M. Whyte and Isaac
P. Howe, conducted the inquest. Howe was the son of a
wealthy Presbyterian minister and farmer who upon his death
had willed over $20,000 to Fulton's Presbyterian church. Isaac
had inherited his farm from his father. Sixty-three years of age
at the time of the inquest, Isaac Howe in 1850 owned land
valued at over $1,600. He also owned six slaves, four males

aged 13 to 52, and two females, aged 35 and 65, some, perhaps all, of whom he continued to hold in 1855. As the probable owner of female slaves, Howe, like William Powell, could hardly have been an objective judicial official. About D. M. Whyte little is known, although his office indicates that he was a man of some means, and very likely also a slaveholder.[9]

The inquest was held after David Newsom filed an affidavit with Whyte and Howe on the morning of June 25. The affidavit charged that David Newsom "has cause to suspect and believe and does suspect and believe that one Negro woman named Celia a Slave of the said Robert Newsom did at the county aforesaid feloniously, willfully and with malice aforethought with a club or some other weapon strike and mortally wound the said Robert Newsom, of which wound or wounds the said Robert Newsom instantly died." Acting upon David Newsom's affidavit, the justices issued a warrant for the arrest of Celia, which was "on the same day executed by bringing the body of said defendant before the court." That same morning Whyte and Howe issued summonses to witnesses, including Harry Newsom and William Powell. Also on the morning of June 25, the justices instructed "any constable" of Fulton Township "to summon six good men and lawful men, householders . . . to appear before us at the late residence of Robert Newsom . . . to inquire how and by whose hands or by what cause he came to his death."[10]

The six-man inquest jury assembled was composed of local residents, men whose lives strikingly resembled that of the murdered Robert Newsom. Their names were George Thomas, Daniel Robinson, John Wells, Simpson Hyton, George Brown, and John Carrington. All had resided in Fulton County at least since the 1850 census. They were typical of Callaway's residents, men of neither wealth nor social status. At fifty-eight the eldest of the group, Daniel Robinson was also the wealthiest. He was not a wealthy man, even by

Callaway standards. Valued at $1,500 his real estate holdings were worth less than half those of Robert Newsom. Two of the men, George Brown, age twenty-five, and Simpson Hyton, age thirty-seven, owned no real property. George Thomas was the only slaveholder of record in 1850, and in that year held four female slaves, an adult and three children. Except for Hyton, who was a wagonmaker, all of the jurymen were farmers.

Like Newsom, the jurors had all come to Missouri from states to the east, bringing their families with them, for all were married. Even the youthful George Brown was not a native Missourian, but was born in Kentucky, as was his wife. Carrington, Hyton, and Thomas had also moved to Missouri from Kentucky; Wells was from Virginia; Robinson from Maryland. The 1850 census indicates that except for Brown, all were fathers. In that year Hyton listed two children, Carrington four, Thomas six, and Wells four. Robinson listed no children, although a young couple lived with him and his wife. The man, Simon Crow, was listed as a farmer and a native of Missouri, and was married to Eveline, age twenty-two, who like Robinson's wife Elizabeth was born in Virginia. In all probability Eveline Crow was the Robinsons' daughter.[11]

Thus the six men who first heard evidence that Celia had killed Robert Newsom were, in practically every respect, his peers. As residents of Fulton Township, it is likely that at least some of the six were also personally acquainted with Newsom and his family, knowing them as neighbors and community members. On that June morning they gathered at the Newsom home to hear three people give testimony about the manner in which he had met his death. The three witnesses, too, were in all probability known personally by at least some, and perhaps all, of the jurors.

The first witness was William Powell, who gave a straightforward account of his questioning of Celia the day before. The only family member to testify was young Coffee Waynescot, who at twelve years of age remained illiterate, unable even to sign his name. Why no adult member of the family testified is puzzling. The most probable explanation is that the evidence of Celia's guilt seemed overwhelming and their testimony did not appear to be necessary. Also, given their shock and grief, it is understandable that they would not testify unless necessary, especially at a pretrial proceeding at which additional corroborating testimony was less essential. The boy briefly and straightforwardly summarized his part in the drama that had unfolded the previous day, and was dismissed. The final witness was Celia, whom the justices called to the stand. Celia's account, like that of Powell and young Waynescot, was brief and to the point. She admitted that she had killed Newsom and disposed of the body in her fireplace. Her testimony added little to the information furnished by Powell and Waynescot, except that she insisted "she did not intend to kill him when she struck him but only wanted to hurt him." Powell's testimony had made it clear that Celia accepted total responsibility for Newsom's death. Powell testified that Celia "said there was no person in the cabin that night but Mr. Robert Newsom and her children, and that she had no assistance in killing him."[12]

The response of the six inquest jurors to the testimony presented was predictable. After hearing the witnesses, the jurors quickly arrived at the finding that there was probable cause to arrest Celia and charge her with the murder of Robert Newsom. Acting upon the jury's verdict, justices Whyte and Howe ordered the constable of Fulton Township to take Celia "and deliver her forthwith to the keeper of the common jail of said County to await her trial at the next term of the Circuit Court of said County."[13]

With Celia formally charged, all that remained was to tidy up some of the details associated with the holding of the inquest. David Newsom, Powell, and probably other potential witnesses were required to post bond to insure their appearance at the circuit court for Celia's trial. Both Powell and Newsom pledged to forfeit to the state of Missouri one hundred dollars in "goods and chattels and tenements and chattels real" if they did not "personally appear before the Circuit Court" during its October term to testify against Celia. Documents summarizing the testimony of the witnesses were drawn up, signed, and attested to by the justices. David Newsom signed with a fine, steady hand, Celia with a mark indicating her illiteracy.

The presiding justices of the peace also confirmed the costs of the inquest, which they forwarded to the justices of the county court. One Felix Nicols was paid eighty-five cents for serving summons to the jurors. Each of the six jurors received mileage costs, which ranged from sixty to seventy-five cents. Whyte and Howe presented the court with their own fees, some five dollars for issuing warrants, swearing the jury, and issuing subpoenas, and an additional request for reimbursement for the cost of travel to and from the Newsom farm. Among the bills submitted by the justices to the county court was a fee of five cents for swearing each witness. In this respect Celia was treated as an equal, as the justices recorded their charge "for swearing Celia a slave $.05."[14]

As Whyte and Howe directed, Celia, now formally charged with murdering her master, was escorted to the county jail in Fulton by the constable of Fulton Township, where she would be lodged until her trial. Her incarceration, however, did not calm the fears of some in the community that there was more to Newsom's murder than the act of an individual slave. The account of the murder in the *Fulton Telegraph* of the following week did little to calm such fears. The paper's report described Newsom as an old man who lived alone. While being visited by relatives, the *Telegraph* reported, Newsom had been attacked and killed by his slave Celia. The paper gave a graphic account of Celia's disposal of Newsom's body, and indicated that the family had first suspected George of the killing. Only after George was questioned, according to the paper was Celia implicated. The correspondent maintained that although Celia confessed to the murder and George insisted that he knew nothing about it, the Newsom family doubted that Celia could have done the deed alone. For some inexplicable reason the *Telegraph*'s account, which was picked up by the Boonville paper, was much less accurate and more alarmist than the account of the murder sent "by correspondent" to the *Missouri Republican* in St. Louis. This account, which lacked the lurid details found in the Fulton paper, made the Newsom kitchen the scene of the crime, but otherwise agreed with the testimony taken at the inquest, with one major exception. The correspondent reported that the murder was committed "without any sufficient cause."[15]

The fact that papers in Missouri towns as far apart as Boonville, roughly forty miles upriver from Fulton, and St. Louis, approximately a hundred miles east of Fulton, carried reports of the murder indicates the level of the white population's concern with slave violence, and especially with the murder of a slaveholder by one of his slaves. The *Fulton Telegraph*'s emphasis upon the fact that the Newsom family continued to suspect George's involvement in the murder also indicates the unease with which slaveholders viewed their human property. There was good reason for the Newsoms to suspect that Celia had not acted alone in the killing of her master. They knew that she and George had been lovers, a relationship that gave George a strong motive for possible complicity in the crime. Because Celia was female, and because she had been ill, had in fact complained of an inability to work because of her illness, they had reason to doubt that, without the aid of another adult, she could have burned Newsom's body in her cabin's fireplace. As is seen below, events that occurred soon after Celia's incarceration demonstrate that not only the Newsoms but others in Fulton and Callaway County were seriously concerned that George and possibly other slaves had taken part in Newsom's murder.

George certainly was aware of and took seriously the suspicions of members of the Newsom family and other members of the white community. In his questioning of George, William Powell had made it clear that the family suspected that he had harmed Newsom, or had helped Celia to do so. If the *Telegraph*'s report that members of the family continued to suspect George's involvement even after Celia's confession is accurate, then there is every reason to believe that their continuing suspicion was conveyed to George. Testimony at Celia's trial also indicates that George continued to be questioned about the possibility of his aiding Celia. Under these circumstances, George would be completely at the mercy of Celia, for if she had implicated him, the family would have certainly believed her. Thus George's safety was directly dependent upon Celia's continued denial of his complicity, a situation of which he must have been fully aware. For George, dependence on Celia must have seemed little protection indeed, since it was he who had first implicated Celia, and because he had helped the family search for Newsom's remains. Because he had experienced the methods of interrogation employed by local whites, George would have known it risky to assume that Celia would continue to deny his involvement, especially if her children were threatened. He also knew that Celia was aware of his actions, of his readiness to assure the Newsoms that it was Celia alone, and not himself, who had killed their father. George, therefore, elected to take matters into his own hands. In a desperate bid to insure that no harm would befall himself, George fled the Newsom farm. His escape only fueled rumors that he had been involved in the murder.[16]

The threat of slave violence and possible insurrection was a specter that constantly haunted the white population of the antebellum South, and the residents of Callaway County were no exception. The fear was there before the United States acquired the land that would become Missouri. President Thomas Jefferson had acquired the Louisiana Purchase from the French when the nation was still in its infancy, only twenty years after the British had acknowledged the futility of continuing their war against American independence. The French had sold this vast region whose magnificent river systems beckoned further European settlement in part because of the very thing Callaway County's residents feared in the summer of 1855, slave rebellion. Inspired by the ideals of the French Revolution, in 1789 Toussaint L'Ouverture, the grandson of an African king, led the half-million slaves of Haiti in a revolt against their some thirty thousand French colonial masters. After more than a decade of struggle and the betrayal, capture, and death of L'Ouverture, the Haitian slaves won independence under the leadership of General Jean-Jacques Dessalines, an ex-slave who in 1804 declared himself emperor of the new nation. In an act of jubilation and revenge, Dessalines's black troops slaughtered many of the whites who remained in Haiti. Some of Haiti's former slaveowners escaped to America, many landing in the southern ports of New Orleans and Charleston. These refugee planters brought with them tales of the unspeakable horrors of slave rebellion. The press spread their stories to guilt-ridden whites throughout the South, who, despite their protestations to the contrary, knew the power of the will to be free and feared it. For white southerners, Haiti became a symbol of that fear. In Virginia, the state from which came many of

54

the early residents of Missouri and Callaway County, among them Robert Newsom and Theodorick Boulware, white fears of the influence of the Haitian slave revolts upon the native black population surfaced as early as 1793. Nearly three decades later, during the debates over Missouri's admission to the Union, southern proponents of admission contended that statehood with slavery would make slave insurrection less likely by insuring that the slave population in the east would never become dangerously disproportionate to the white population. Northern opponents countered that statehood with slavery could lead to Haitian-like revolts in Missouri. That the white population of Callaway County shared these fears is evident from reports of black violence against former masters in the West Indies carried by the *Fulton Telegraph* as late as 1848.[17]

A decade after Missouri joined the Union and approximately a decade before Celia's birth, Nat Turner's rebellion heightened the fear of slave rebellion that Haiti had instilled in the hearts of white southerners. In August 1831, a slave preacher on a Southampton County, Virginia, plantation led an uprising of a handful of slaves. In one terrible day of vengeance a merciless Nat and his followers murdered more than fifty whites—plantation masters and their families, men, women, and children. News of the rebellion flashed through the South, and within a matter of days Nat Turner was transformed into a symbol of rebellion, the personification of a terror that was to be guarded against at all cost. Given the large number of Virginians who had migrated to Missouri and Callaway County in the two decades following Nat Turner's rebellion, there is statistically a high probability that among the county's white residents in 1855 were individuals who had been in Virginia during the events of the Turner rebellion. Any of Callaway's citizens who had been in Virginia in 1831 would have retained personal memories of the sense of panic that had gripped the state; of the preparations for war against the slave population taken by Virginia's governor, John Floyd; of the bloody reckoning as militia units hunted down, tortured, and killed the rebels and other slaves merely suspected of being their accomplices.[18]

White Missourians' fear of slave plots was no mere fantasy. In 1850 a group of some thirty slaves in western Missouri had armed themselves with knives, clubs, and three guns and attempted to escape. Overtaken by a heavily armed posse, the slaves surrendered only after their leader was shot dead. The rise of the abolitionist movement had convinced southerners that northern abolitionists were a constant threat to their slave property and would go to any lengths to support planned escapes and insurrections. In Missouri this fear was heightened with the passage of the Kansas-Nebraska Act of 1854, and the struggle for Kansas between Free Soil and proslavery forces that followed. Slaveholding Missourians came to view all nonslaveholding Kansas settlers as abolitionists and "nigger stealers," ideologues who threatened both the property and safety of law-abiding Missouri citizens. Shortly after Celia killed Newsom, for example, tales of the efforts of an Irish abolitionist named Martin Gallagher and a Methodist minister, W. H. Wylie, to aid an escape plot surfaced in Cash County. At a public meeting attended by some two hundred angry residents, Wylie was denounced for his role in the supposed plot and given seven days to leave the county. Wylie accepted the crowd's suggestion.[19]

And so in the summer of 1855 in Callaway County it is little wonder that rumors that Celia had an accomplice or accomplices in the murder of Robert Newsom persisted for over a week after her arrest. Nor is it strange that the persistent rumors alarmed a number of individuals in the white community other than members of the Newsom family. In fact, despite Celia's insistence that she alone and unaided killed Newsom and disposed of his body, there was considerable circumstantial evidence to the contrary. George remained the logical suspect as her accomplice, and his escape provided a strong piece of circumstantial evidence implicating him in either the murder or the disposal of the body. Although Celia never implicated George, the fact that when questioned by William Powell she gave at least two versions of what happened in her cabin on the night Newsom was killed lent weight to suppositions that George had participated in the actual murder. The physical difficulties of burning a human body in a cabin fireplace within the period of time between approximately midnight and sunrise also supported speculation that Celia had received assistance. To alone dispose of the body in this manner, Celia would have had to build a fire hot enough to burn the body, place the corpse in the flames and keep it there, and maintain the fire at a temperature high enough to consume Newsom's flesh and reduce even his bones to a state of brittleness that allowed them to be crushed by a heavy object. Accomplishing all this would have taxed the strength of a healthy woman, and Celia was pregnant and sick. Finally, the fact that Celia's children were in the cabin posed a problem. The stench of burning human flesh within the confines of the cabin, combined with the heat from the flames, surely would have aroused the children. Tending to two small children unaided while burning Newsom's remains would have presented Celia with an extremely difficult task.

Lingering concerns within the community about the manner in which Newsom met his death finally led some to seek more definitive answers to questions suggested by Celia's confession. Several Callaway citizens eventually prevailed upon William T. Snell, the county sheriff, to allow Celia to be questioned further about possible accomplices. Snell, elected in 1854, had served less than a year in office and undoubtedly wished to do everything possible to enhance his chances of reelection the following year.[20] He agreed that Celia could be examined by two individuals, Thomas Shoatman and Jefferson Jones, "to ascertain whether she had any accomplices in the crime."[21]

Jones was by far the more significant of Celia's new inquisitors. The 1850 census records portray Thomas Shoatman as a man of few means. Then thirty-nine years old, Shoatman, a wagoner, owned neither real property nor slaves. He had moved from Virginia with wife and child sometime after 1836. By 1850, he had fathered six children, ranging in age from two to fourteen. Jones, on the other hand, was an up and coming young lawyer. By marriage the nephew of John Jameson, Jones had moved to Callaway County from Kentucky with his father in 1840. Three years later he began to practice law in Fulton and soon became one of the town's leading attorneys. Active in politics, he stumped for Jameson in the 1844 congressional campaign, an act of family loyalty since Jones was a Whig. In 1848 he served as a Whig elector from Missouri and was offered and declined the Whig nomination for a legislative seat in 1852. In 1855 he was a man of some wealth, and had two children, a son eight and a daughter six. It is also highly probable that in 1855 Jones owned several slaves, including a female slave of approximately Celia's age, since in 1850 he held three slaves, one a female twenty-two years of age, and in 1860 he held ten slaves, including females age twenty-six and twenty-four.[22] Thus Jones, like Celia's earlier inquisitors, would have had a keen personal interest in the responses he received.

Like others who had questioned Celia, Jones used a rather direct approach. He first asked Celia "whether she thought she would be hung for what she had done." Upon receiving a positive reply, Jones "then told her she should tell the whole truth." From Jones's testimony it appears that Celia fully complied with his request, and that once she began her story, she required no prompting by additional questions.

She gave a detailed account of her original confrontation with Newsom, his insistence upon continued sexual favors, her striking and killing her master, and the manner in which she disposed of the body. At no point, however, did Celia implicate George or any other slave in the crime. Not satisfied with her response, Jones resumed his questioning, specifically inquiring about the possibility that others were involved in Newsom's death. He asked her "whether she had told anyone that she intended to kill the old man." Celia replied that she never had.

Disappointed once again with Celia's reply, Jones adopted a new tactic. He informed Celia "that George had run off." By delivering this piece of information, Jones clearly sought to break Celia's spirit, to impress upon her that, whatever her relationship with George had been in the past, she was now abandoned by him and totally alone. Having informed Celia of George's escape, Jones then told her "that she might as well tell if he had anything to do with killing the old man." Despite Jones's news, which must have come as a psychological blow even though Celia knew George had previously implicated her in the murder, once again Celia denied that George had had any involvement in Newsom's death. Jones continued to press the issue. He asked Celia "if George had advised her to kill the old man." For the third time Celia denied that George had in any way influenced her actions. Still not satisfied, Jones suggested that Celia could not possibly have killed Newsom in the manner she described. Instead, he contended, what actually occurred was that George had "struck the old man from behind" and killed him. To this suggestion Celia's response was even more emphatic. George, she replied, had not struck the old man, knew nothing of Newsom's death, and was not at her cabin at any time of the night on which Newsom was killed.[23] The most logical conclusion to be drawn from the evidence is that Celia told Jones the truth, despite the circumstantial evidence to the contrary. On the other hand, if Celia's categorical denial of George's involvement was untrue, it was a remarkable expression of her devotion to him.

Whether Celia's fourth, and emphatic, denial convinced Jefferson Jones that neither George nor anyone else had helped her kill Newsom cannot be ascertained from the evidence. What is clear is that Jones stopped his questioning at this point, probably convinced either that Celia was telling the truth or that it was unlikely that she would implicate George or anyone else under any circumstances. The "several citizens" who had insisted upon his "convening" with Celia would simply have to be content with the results of his interrogation. The lack of additional stories from Fulton and Callaway County about Celia and the Newsom murder in the papers of nearby Boonville and Jefferson City, or in the Columbia and St. Louis press, suggests that those who had prompted Jones's interrogation were satisfied with the results. Since copies of the *Fulton Telegraph* for 1855 are no longer extant, the degree to which members of the community continued to express concern about Newsom's death also cannot be documented.

The rather curious response of Harry Newsom to press reports of his father's murder, on the other hand, is a matter of record. The account of his father's death carried by the *Missouri Republican* of St. Louis, which inaccurately reported that the crime had been committed in the kitchen of the Newsom home, greatly disturbed Harry Newsom. The reporter had probably assumed that the kitchen had been the scene of the crime because the body had been destroyed in a fireplace. This lack of accuracy prompted an angry letter to the *Republican* from Harry. He carefully explained that the murder had occurred in Celia's cabin, "some fifty yards from the house," not in the kitchen of the family home. He expressed the hope that the *Republican* would correct this error, "in justice to the family." He accepted as correct, however, the *Republican*'s assertion that Robert Newsom had been murdered "without any sufficient cause."[24] Harry Newsom's reasons for failing to correct the *Republican*'s inaccurate statement about Celia's motive are readily apparent. After all, he was unlikely to wish the general public to know that his father routinely sexually exploited his young female slave. His insistence that the erroneous identification of the crime scene be corrected is also understandable, although it posed some problems. What Harry seems to have wished to accomplish was to make clear that no other family members were involved in the incident, hence his appeal for "justice to the family." Yet by calling attention to the fact that his father was killed not in his home but in Celia's cabin, he also raised the issue of why Robert Newsom was in a slave cabin on the night of his murder, an issue that Harry chose to ignore. Whatever his reasons, Harry Newsom's response to the *Republican*, with its emphasis upon facts and its total disregard for motive, anticipated the approach the prosecuting attorney would adopt during Celia's trial.

Four

Backdrop

Indicted for Newsom's murder on June 25, Celia would spend the remainder of the summer in the Callaway County jail awaiting her October trial. As she waited through the summer heat, the citizens of Callaway and Missouri who would conduct her trial and determine her fate were being drawn into yet another emotionally charged debate over slavery and its future in the neighboring Kansas Territory. As in 1820 and 1850, the debate raged across the nation, its volume and intensity reaching levels that frightened many who had previously paid scant attention to the morality of slavery. In Missouri the debate acquired an even more strident, threatening tone, and eventually plunged the state into violence that threatened its citizens with civil war. Slavery captured the interest of the state's press, as papers in St. Louis, Columbia, Jefferson City, and other communities devoted column after column to the escalating clash of opinions about slavery within state and nation. As the year progressed, news accounts and editorials alike presented little hope that the debate would remain peaceful in either Missouri or the country. The pages of the *Fulton Telegraph* reflected this increasing concern over the issue of slavery, indicating that the citizens of Fulton and Callaway County were fully aware of the mounting seriousness of the controversy. Coverage of the slavery issue in the *Telegraph* and other local Missouri papers indicates that the white population of Callaway County, including those individuals who would eventually compose the jury impaneled for Celia's October trial, were themselves caught up in the emotional fervor of the slavery debates.[1]

Senator Stephen Douglas of Illinois had insured that the people of Callaway County would be more than ordinarily concerned about slavery in the summer in which Celia was tried for her life. He had not intended to plunge the nation into a wrenching examination of the morality of slavery, or to throw the people of Missouri into a dither about the nature of the institution and its future prospects. Through the Kansas-Nebraska Act of the previous year, he sought only to organize additional territories that lay west of Missouri in the old Louisiana Purchase so that the nation could proceed with the business of constructing a transcontinental railroad, preferably one with its eastern terminus in Chicago. To enhance its chance of adoption, Douglas championed a bill that repealed the old Missouri Compromise and allowed the possibility of the expansion of slavery into the new federal territories of Kansas and Nebraska, which the proposed legislation would create. Douglas also proposed this legislation in part to bolster his chances of capturing the Democratic presidential nomination, which would have required strong support from the South. Like other northern Democrats who did not view slavery as an essentially moral issue, Douglas woefully underestimated the opposition to the bill among average northern citizens, most of whom had reached the conclusion that slavery was neither morally acceptable nor in their economic interest. While most were willing to allow their white southern brethren to continue the practice, they were not prepared to see the institution spread into territories from which it had been barred by an agreement accepted by southerners for some three decades.

Northern anger over the Kansas–Nebraska Act and the role of Democrats in securing its passage launched the Republican party in the congressional elections of 1854. To many northerners, abolitionists and nonabolitionists alike, the bill's enactment represented a challenge from the slaveholding South, one to which they were determined to respond. On the Senate floor William Seward expressed the thoughts of millions of his fellow citizens when he accepted the perceived challenge from the South "in behalf of the cause of freedom." The citizenry of the free states, he promised, stood ready to "engage in competition for the virgin soil of Kansas, and God give victory to the side which is stronger in numbers as it is in the right."[2]

Seward's words were no idle threat. Even before the Kansas–Nebraska bill won Congressional approval, Eli Thayer and others had organized the Massachusetts Emigrant Aid Company. Capitalized at $5 million, the company, which later became the New England Emigrant Aid Company, sought "to aid and protect emigrants from New England or from the Old World in settling in the West." Thayer and other company leaders sought to insure that Kansas be peopled by Free-Soilers, emigrants dedicated to the family farm and the exclusion of slavery. The concept was not limited to New England, and other emigrant aid associations quickly sprang up in New York and Ohio. Thayer and his associates lost no time implementing their settlement plans, although their fundraising efforts fell far short of expectations. Settlers financed by the New England Emigrant Aid Company began to arrive in Kansas as early as August 1854, less than three months after the passage of the Kansas–Nebraska Act.[3]

Predictably, southerners were outraged by the efforts of the Emigrant Aid Company to see Kansas settled by Free-Soilers. As another slave state, Kansas would continue the balance of slave and free state representation in the Senate so vital to the South's ability to protect its peculiar institution. Sentiments against the "diabolical schemes" and "fanatical army" of the New England Emigrant Aid Company ran high in Missouri, encouraged by the demagogic oratory of David R. Atchinson. Locked in a struggle for control of the state's Democratic party with congressman and former senator Thomas Hart Benton, who personally opposed any further expansion of slavery into the territories, Atchinson saw the Kansas issue as an opportunity to consolidate Missouri's proslavery Democrats and retain his Senate seat, which Benton sought to recapture.

A Kentucky native and graduate of Transylvania University, in 1830 the flamboyant Atchinson arrived in Liberty, Missouri, soon after being admitted to the bar. In 1840 he moved to Platte City in Platte County, where he became the ardent champion of the proslavery forces in western Missouri. As early as the summer of 1854 Atchinson had written Jefferson Davis that within six months there would be "the Devil to pay in Kansas and in this State. We are organizing to meet [New England's] organization. We will be compelled to shoot, burn and hang, but the thing will soon be over." True to his word, Atchinson, aided by such prominent Missouri Democrats as Benjamin F. Stringfellow, began to convert rhetoric into action. Stringfellow, also a lawyer, migrated to Missouri in 1838, and soon became active in politics as an anti-Benton Democrat. Moving to Weston in Platte County in 1853, he surpassed even Atchinson in the rashness of his verbal assaults upon the abolitionist enemy. Throughout 1854, Atchinson and Stringfellow labored to create an organized resistance to the perceived abolitionist threat in both Kansas and Missouri, forming "self protection" socities throughout southern and western Missouri. Given such colorful names as the "Blue Lodges" and "Sons of the South," these organizations were composed of members eager to follow Atchinson's call to action. Meanwhile, Benton, whose support was strongest in the St. Louis region, sought to counter Atchinson's emotional appeals.[4]

Throughout 1855, Atchinson continued his crusade to make Kansas a slave state and to retain control of Missouri's Democratic party in the process. The year began with a donnybrook in the state legislature over Atchinson's expiring Senate seat. The candidacy of a proslavery Whig, Alexander W. Doniphan, denied a majority to either Benton or Atchinson. After forty-one ballots and weeks of furious political infighting, the deadlock persisted. The legislature decided to leave the seat vacant, and after passing motions to meet again in November, adjourned on March 5.[5]

Determined to retain his Senate seat, Atchinson immediately set about to enhance his reputation as Missouri's leading proslavery advocate by using his supporters to control territorial elections in Kansas. Border ruffians from Missouri had streamed into Kansas in November of 1854 for the election of the territory's congressional delegate. Their votes had elected John W. Whitfield, Indian agent and Atchinson's old friend. Atchinson's supporters once again crossed over into Kansas for the territory's legislative elections, held March 30, 1855. The Missourians swept proslavery legislators into power in Kansas, bullying at the polls suspected Free-Soil voters with curses, threats of violence and occasional rifle fire. Atchinson boasted: "We had at least seven thousand men in the territory . . . and one third of them will remain there. . . . The pro-slavery ticket prevailed everywhere. . . . Now let the Southern men come on with their slaves. . . . We are playing for a mighty stake; if we win we carry slavery to the Pacific Ocean."[6]

Within weeks after the Kansas legislative elections, and at approximately the same time that Celia conceived her third child, Atchinson's followers brought their campaign of violence to bear against their opponents in Missouri. On April 14, Blue Lodge members rode into Parkville, located in Platte County across the Missouri River from Leavenworth. They came to silence the *Parkville Industrial Luminary*, a paper highly critical of the border ruffians' vigilante tactics. A body of armed men entered the paper's office, seized the press and type and carried them into the street. Members of the mob read resolutions declaring the paper's editors, George S. Park and W. J. Patterson, traitors to the South and proclaiming that if found, they would be tarred, feathered, and shot. Mob leaders issued a warning that Park and Patterson were to leave town within three weeks. Should the editors flee to Kansas, the mob pledged "our honor as men to follow and hang them wherever we can take them." Its warning delivered, the mob marched to the Missouri River under a "Boston Aid" banner and threw the press into its waters. Warned of the impending attack by a friend, Park watched from hiding the destruction of his press. Not so fortunate, Patterson was discovered by the mob, which sent up a cry to drown him in the river. Only the fact of his Canadian citizenship persuaded the mob that his life should be spared. Its destruction of the press complete, the mob spared Patterson's life and released the editor with a stern warning to abandon his abolitionist views, depart town, or face a decidedly bleak future. The Parkville raid created something of a furor when reports of it reached the northern press, and the ruffians who had participated in it were roundly denounced by Horace Greeley of the *New York Tribune* and other editors.[7]

During the exact period in which Celia contemplated what to do about her pregnancy and George's resulting ultimatum, from early April until the end of June, the public furor in

Missouri over slavery and Kansas seemed to subside. Yet tensions remained just beneath the surface, and the proslavery Missouri press periodically issued warnings of the abolitionist threat in Kansas. On June 21, just two days before Celia killed Robert Newsom, for example, Boonville's *Dollar Missouri Journal* reported "an informant's" view that abolitionists in Lawrence planned to organize, steal slaves in Kansas, then invade and colonize Missouri with a black army. Meanwhile, the continued plotting of Atchinson and others to insure both his return to the Senate and the spread of slavery into Kansas embroiled Missourians in yet another round of furious debates over slavery, one which lasted throughout the summer months during which Celia sat in a Fulton jail waiting to be tried for her life.[8]

While residents of Missouri's western counties, along the Kansas border, were the most ardent proponents of slavery and its expansion into the territories, by late May slavery dominated local polities in the state's central counties. For example, in Boone County, which bordered Callaway to the west, conservatives viewed with alarm the efforts of "Atchinson and his Mobocrats" to do "all in their power to get up excitement in this locality," including conducting public meetings to address the issues of slavery and Kansas. Such local meetings were part of a larger plan. Seeking to bolster Atchinson's campaign to retain his Senate seat, several of his supporters met in Lexington on June 21 and issued a statement addressed to the state legislature and "all true friends of the South and the Union." They announced a convention to be held on July 12, in Lexington, to develop measures "for our protection against aggression on our slave property" by abolitionists in Kansas, and to consider a "proper Southern response" to the "alarming state of affairs existing in our Country." This call for a convention prompted yet another flurry of emotional editorials on slavery and Kansas in the state's press, and in many communities tempers flared at local "conventions" held to elect representatives to the Lexington gathering.[9] Thus, the intensified slavery debates in Missouri coincided precisely with the investigation of Robert Newsom's murder, and the significance of the slavery issue in the politics of neighboring Boone County strongly suggests that residents of Callaway would have been equally concerned.

Within days after the residents of Callaway County learned of Celia's indictment, and at approximately the same time that Jefferson Jones was permitted to question Celia about possible accomplices, the slavery controversy in Missouri became yet more heated. On July 9, James Shannon, president of the University of Missouri, entered the debate with an ardent defense of slavery and a provocative attack upon the abolitionists. President of the university for five years, Shannon, an Irish-born Presbyterian educated at the University of Belfast, had arrived in Missouri after service on the faculties of the University of Georgia and Bacon College in Kentucky. With his strong proslavery views, he had soon run afoul of the Benton faction of the state's Democratic party, and Benton had tried and failed to obtain his dismissal as early as 1852. As the slavery debates heated up in 1854, Shannon again came under attack from Bentonites for his increasing tendency to become actively involved in politics, especially his support of Atchinson's efforts to protect slavery by insuring its spread into Kansas.[10]

In his "card," sent to all of Missouri's newspapers, the fiery Shannon attacked those who called him a bigoted, fanatical madman and political priest. "High motives of patriotism and regard for the salvation of the lost world" impelled him to speak out. It was his duty, he declared, to counter abolitionist teachings, so as not to "corrupt the minds of students committed to my trust." Far from being the evil abolitionists claimed, slavery was "sanctioned alike by the Bible, the Laws of Nature, and the Constitution of the United States," and Congress had neither the authority nor the right to "impair a vested interest in slaves in the territories, the District of Columbia, or anywhere on earth." "Unless the swelling tide of anti-slavery fanaticism be beaten back," Shannon predicted with prescient accuracy, the bonds of Union would break within five years.[11]

Shannon's card hit Missouri like a thunderclap. In St. Louis the *Intelligencer* and the *Democrat* railed against Shannon, as did Columbia's *Statesman*. On the other hand, the *Missouri Republican*, also a St. Louis paper, the *Jefferson Examiner*, the *Southwest Democrat* and Columbia's *Dollar Missouri Journal* supported him. Shannon himself embarked on a speaking tour, addressing crowds of up to a thousand, and arranged to be a featured speaker at the Lexington convention. Indeed, the timing of the release of Shannon's "card" suggests that he was, as critics charged, part of an orchestrated campaign to use the Lexington convention to crush the Bentonites and place Missouri solidly behind Atchinson's proslavery programs.[12]

On July 12, the proslavery convention met in Lexington, as scheduled. The delegates represented twenty-six counties, with most coming from the large slaveholding counties, especially those located along the Missouri and across from Kansas. Callaway, despite its large slaveholding population, was not represented, and seventeen other counties with significant slave populations also failed to send representatives, an indication that many sympathetic to slavery saw the convention as an event to promote Atchinson. St. Louis, Benton's stronghold, sent as delegates two individuals the *Daily Democrat* denounced as unrepresentative of the feelings of either the city or county. Despite the proslavery sentiments of the delegates, Atchinson did not go unchallenged at the convention, for Alexander Doniphan attended, as did Governor Sterling Price, whose name also had been entered in the senatorial contest of the preceding January.[13]

James Shannon delivered the convention's opening address, which set the tone for the two-day event. His remarks were nothing if not unequivocal. Any threat to the biblically sanctioned right to hold slaves, Shannon assured his audience, "is just cause of war between the separate states." Those who advocated restrictions on slavery he denounced as "liars, yelping curs, assassins, knaves, Negro thieves and horse thieves."[14]

After listening to speaker after speaker berate abolitionists and condemn their efforts to undermine slavery and incorporate Kansas into the Union as a free state, convention delegates adopted a series of resolutions on July 13. The resolutions declared slavery, in every aspect, a matter of state concern; pronounced efforts to stop the admission of Kansas as a slave state hostile to the Constitution and the Compromise of 1850; approved the Kansas-Nebraska Act; and condemned abolitionists for recruiting and sending settlers to Kansas with the purpose of abolishing slavery in Missouri. The resolutions expressed the fears of slaveholders who held slave property valued in excess of $25 million that their property would be threatened if "hired fanatics" controlled Kansas. The resolutions called upon the people of Missouri to take all measures "suitable and just" to "stop this threat," and appealed to northerners to cease all support of emigrant aid societies.[15]

The proslavery convention met with predictable reactions. The Bentonite press found its resolutions absurd and considered the affair as simply another of Atchinson's political machinations. The St. Louis *Daily Democrat*, for example, saw the gathering as evidence of Atchinson's "treasonable designs . . . to incite a civil war in our midst by riot and bloodshed and trespass against the laws and constitution of the country." The paper was almost as hard on Doniphan, who, it noted, had attended the convention to stake out his position as the Whig's proslavery senatorial candidate. The *Dollar Missouri Journal* and the *Missouri Republican*, on the other hand, praised the convention's work. The *Republican* was particularly laudatory, proclaiming that all "Union loving" people would endorse the resolutions without reservation, and that the convention had placed Missouri "in her right position before the country."[16]

The general furor over the slavery issue created throughout Missouri by the Lexington proslavery convention and President Shannon's card in defense of slavery, especially the widespread press coverage of both events, indicate that the *Fulton Telegraph* kept the people of Fulton and Callaway County fully apprised of both developments. Given the state of political turmoil that existed, it is also likely that these events exerted some influence over Celia's trial. Both the convention and the issuance of Shannon's card had occurred within two weeks after Celia had been indicted and jailed for Robert Newsom's murder. It was inevitable, given the local publicity her crime had received, that Celia's situation would have been on the minds of Callaway citizens even as they contemplated the moral and legal issues raised by the slavery debates.

The concerns about slavery entertained by the people of Missouri and Callaway County did not cease once the proslavery convention adjourned. To insure that the slavery issue remained before the public, President Shannon embarked on a statewide speaking tour, bringing his message of alarm directly to Missouri's communities. Shannon's messianic efforts were finally halted by the legislature in December of 1855. The legislators adopted a measure that reduced the president's salary if his official duties were not discharged because of protracted absence from the university. The political maneuverings of Atchinson, Benton, and Doniphan did not stop. Each man continued his struggle to gain Atchinson's Senate seat, which expired at the end of the year. In the fierce struggle that ensued, Atchinson's proslavery rhetoric intensified, and in both Washington and Missouri he redoubled his efforts to impose slavery upon Kansas. He had determined to make Kansas a symbol of the South's demand that slavery be protected in the federal territories, to insure that slavery be allowed the opportunity to expand.[17]

During the remainder of 1855, additional vigilante committees and patrols were organized throughout Missouri. Encouraged by the words and actions of Atchinson and his lieutenants, including B. F. Stringfellow and Colonel A. G. Boone of Westport, proslavery advocates in Missouri's southern and western counties organized into paramilitary units whose members openly talked of invading Kansas to eliminate abolitionists and "nigger stealers." Such groups were also needed, one paper explained, "for the purpose of purging their communities of Abolitionism, and for the more thorough discipline of the slave population."[18]

With vigilante groups active in so many of the state's counties, occasional outbreaks of violence related to the slavery issue were predictable. Missouri continued to be plagued by such episodes, just as did Kansas, although in Missouri the violence rarely was carried directly into the political process. Rather, much of the violence was directed against those individuals suspected of abolitionist sentiments. In Forley, Missouri, for example, "Atchinson and Stringfellow Ruffians" forced their way into a Methodist church service and threatened to kill the minister on the spot. The armed mob spared the minister's life only because of the pleas of the congregation. The attack caused some Methodist ministers to flee the region, and prompted others known to hold antislavery sentiments to carry handguns. Travelers on the Missouri River whose credentials were questionable came in for rough treatment. In one incident, a group of angry Missourians attacked a minister from Maine who was returning by riverboat from a tour of Kansas. Members of the mob beat the man about the head with a chair while the passengers urged his assailants to "kill the abolitionist nigger stealer, kill the dough-faced son of a bitch." The minister, defenders of the mob's action asserted, deserved his fate for "loudly preaching the higher law doctrine" and saying "the Negro was, in every particular, as good as the white man," and should have equal rights. In some counties vigilantes rounded up and jailed persons suspected of abolitionist views. Some suspects received rougher treatment than others. In Weston, near the Kansas border, a drunken proslavery mob abducted a lawyer from Leavenworth named Phillips, tarred and feathered him, then had a slave conduct an "auction" at which Phillips was sold to the highest bidder. The Weston border ruffians eventually spared the man's life and allowed his brother to return him to Leavenworth.[19]

In Kansas, slavery became the pervasive political issue, overwhelming all other considerations, with proslavery and free state forces both determined to capture the territorial government. Throughout the summer and early fall of 1855 the political struggle in Kansas grew more intense, and supporters of both camps began arming themselves for what seemed an inevitable showdown. Missourians received blow-by-blow accounts of the struggle for control of Kansas in the pages of the Missouri press, and each event in Kansas had its repercussions in Missouri, especially in the western border and large slaveholding counties.

Although free state forces besieged Governor Andrew Reeder with requests that he nullify the results of the March Kansas elections in which Missourians had helped elect a proslavery territorial legislature, the governor refused to do so. He did, however, call for new elections on May 22 in several counties where evidence of fraud was incontrovertible, and as a result several free state advocates were elected. On July 2, the proslavery Kansas legislature met at Pawnee, just as Atchinson, James Shannon, and others were preparing for their proslavery convention in Lexington. The territorial legislature immediately upped the ante in the struggle for Kansas. In a direct challenge to Reeder, the legislature expelled all of the free state delegates chosen in the special May election, and gave their seats to proslavery representatives. The legislature overrode Reeder's veto of this travesty, and on July 16 moved to Shawnee Mission, immediately across the river from Kansas City and the border ruffians of Missouri.

Unburdened of their free state opposition, the proslavery legislators then proceeded to enact the so-called "bogus laws," including an almost verbatim copy of Missouri's slave codes. To insure that proslavery forces would control all subsequent elections, members enacted legislation allowing any man present at the polls on election day to vote as long as he swore to support the Fugitive Slave Act of 1850 and pay a dollar poll tax. Outraged by these actions, the heretofore compliant Reeder denounced the proslavery legislature as a body of renegades, declaring their enactments illegal. The governor's efforts to curb the proslavery forces drew immediate opposition from southern democrats, including Atchinson, who convinced President Franklin Pierce that Reeder should be replaced. Antislavery forces believed that Pierce had acted upon the advice of his secretary of war, Jefferson Davis, although Davis denied the charge. On July 31, Pierce withdrew Reeder's commission, and on August 15 the president appointed in his stead William Shannon, a proslavery Democrat and former governor of Ohio who as a congressman in 1854 had supported the Kansas-Nebraska Act.[20]

The campaign of intimidation waged by proslavery forces in Kansas and their Missouri supporters failed to subdue Free Soil advocates, who represented a numerical majority among actual settlers in the territory. They were determined to create a territorial government representative of Kansas settlers, rather than the politics of Missouri's border ruffians. Throughout the summer and early fall of 1855, Free Soil forces organized to challenge the proslavery territorial government. Political direction was furnished by James Lane, a former Democratic congressman from Indiana who had supported the Kansas-Nebraska bill but recognized in the Free Soil movement a chance to rejuvenate his political career; Charles Robinson, a Massachusetts native and agent of the New England Emigrant Aid Company; and Andrew Reeder, by now thoroughly disgusted with the proslavery policies of the Pierce administration. Efforts to organize an opposition party began when Robinson delivered an impassioned speech in Lawrence, headquarters for the Emigrant Aid Company in Kansas, on the Fourth of July. Robinson urged resistance to the efforts of Missouri's border ruffians to subvert the spirit of the Declaration of Independence and force slavery upon Kansas against the wishes of the citizenry. He also urged the formation of two military companies, to be armed with two hundred Sharps rifles and two field guns. The increased determination of Free Soil forces to resist, with arms if necessary, the proslavery government elected by the vote of Missouri border ruffians touched off a northern campaign to raise funds for the purchase of Sharps rifles to send to Kansas. Within weeks, wagonloads of repeating rifles began to pour into the disputed territory.[21]

Robinson's speech also provided the impetus for a series of July meetings of Free Soil advocates at Lawrence, including the expelled free state members of the territorial legislature. At a mid-August meeting at Shawnee Mission, antislavery forces called for a convention on September 5 at Big Springs to organize a free state party. Directed by Lane, Reeder, and Robinson, the Big Springs convention marked a turning point in the struggle for Kansas. Convention delegates repudiated the authority of the proslavery territorial legislature and called for yet another gathering in Topeka on September 19 to determine the feasibility of holding a constitutional convention. They also created the Free State party, and adopted a party platform. While creating an institution through which to pursue their fight against the expansion of slavery into Kansas, convention delegates offered little solace to blacks. Rather, delegates adopted a party platform that advocated the eventual exclusion from Kansas of all blacks, free or slave. The convention also nominated Andrew Reeder as the Free State party's congressional candidate and set October 9 as the date for congressional elections. With the Big Springs convention, free state advocates served notice to the proslavery territorial government that they intended to create their own territorial government, one which would claim both the moral and legal right to govern Kansas.[22]

As expected by both camps, the Free State party convention delegates who gathered in Topeka on September 19 acted to further consolidate opposition to the proslavery territorial government. Under the tutelage of James Lane, the convention did much more than simply issue a call for a formal constitutional convention to convene in Topeka on October 23. The delegates created a territorial executive committee, chaired by Lane, which was to act as a free state provisional government. The committee was also empowered to plan a strategy that would result in Kansas's entrance into the union as a free state. Delegates chose Lane to chair yet another crucial committee, "the committee on an address to the people," which was charged with justifying the convention's actions to the public.

The Topeka convention only heightened tensions between the two camps. Proslavery forces in Kansas once again appealed for help from Missouri's increasingly well-organized border ruffians. Atchinson and other ruffian leaders responded. Once more Missourians crossed into Kansas and, in a calculated repudiation of their adversaries' call for a free state constitutional convention, overwhelmingly reelected J. W. Whitfield as the territory's congressional representative in an election

held on October 1, one week before Celia's trial was scheduled to begin. Free state forces, who boycotted the October 1 congressional election, marched to the polls as scheduled on October 9, the exact date on which Celia entered
the Callaway County courthouse to be tried for the murder
of Robert Newsom. They voted overwhelmingly to send
Andrew Reeder to Congress as their territorial representative.
Kansas now had two governments, each claiming to represent
the will of the people, and two congressional representatives,
each claiming legitimacy. Free state forces were prepared to
draft a constitution and apply for entrance into the Union
as a free state while the Pierce administration continued to
recognize the proslavery territorial government. The threat of
open civil strife loomed ominously on the territory's political
horizon, attracting fanatics of both camps. On the night of
October 6 John Brown arrived in Kansas to join his sons,
already encamped there, his wagon loaded with rifles and
swords.[23]

Thus on the eve of Celia's trial, the reverberations of an
increasingly violent struggle over slavery in Kansas had disrupted the public tranquility in Missouri and threatened with
discord the state's basic political, legal, and social institutions.
Armed vigilantes held sway in many counties, physically
intimidating anyone who voiced antislavery opinions. The
state's leading politicians were locked in a struggle for a United
States Senate seat, with Atchison's forces determined to use
the Kansas issue and an impassioned defense of slavery to
retain it. The state's proslavery press was filled with intem-
perate editorials denouncing abolitionists as an immediate
threat to the expansion of slavery into Kansas and to the
continued existence of slavery in Missouri. The northern
press periodically carried items on the turmoil within the
state, a fact of which Missourians were painfully aware,
and many resented. A rejoinder by a proslavery Missouri

editor was typical. Abolitionists, he wrote, should leave the South alone. They should instead respect the federal law and Constitution, both of which recognized and protected slavery. Northern citizens should see that federal fugitive slave laws were faithfully carried out, rather than opposed by bayonet, as was the case in Boston.[24] Under such circumstances the slavery debates, which threatened so alarmingly the domestic tranquility of both Missouri and the nation, were inevitably a part of the backdrop to Celia's trial, scheduled for October 9, 1855.

Five

The Trial

To Judge William Augustus Hall fell the lot of presiding over Celia's trial. Born in Portland, Maine, in 1815, Hall had moved as a child to a small northern Virginia town on the Potomac River. He spent the remainder of his boyhood in Harper's Ferry before departing for Yale. After college, in 1840 Hall accompanied his father's family on yet another move, this time to Randolph County, Missouri. There he studied law and was admitted to the bar in 1841. He opened a practice in Huntsville, which he later moved to Fayette. The young and ambitious attorney quickly entered the ranks of those active in Democratic party politics. In 1847 the party rewarded his efforts by nominating him for a circuit court judgeship. Hall won the election and held the position until the outbreak of the Civil War. A Benton Democrat, Hall had strong Unionist sentiments and in 1861 abandoned the bench to accept a congressional seat left vacant by the expulsion of Confederate supporter John B. Clark.[1]

Hall's Unionist sentiments carried significant implications for Celia's trial, for under Missouri law slaves accused of capital crimes were entitled to a court-appointed attorney. A judge's views about slavery, an issue at that moment the subject of such furious debate among Missourians, could, in fact, be crucial. A judge with proslavery sympathies, one supportive of the stance of Atchinson, Shannon, and others on the issues of Kansas and slavery, might have selected a defense attorney who shared his political convictions. Under such conditions, Celia would have been given a perfunctory defense, convicted, and executed.

While Hall's views about slavery are unknown, his Unionist leanings, coupled with the fact that he held an elected position, indicate that in the summer of 1855 he would have been keenly aware of the slavery issue and its significance to both Missouri and the nation. Hall also probably understood that the trial held at least some potential to contribute to the ongoing national debate over slavery. The abolitionist press was full of tales of the brutality of slaveholders, and was particularly fond of stories that involved the sexual abuse of female slaves by their masters. Handled badly, Celia's trial could provide additional grist for the propaganda mill of the northern abolitionists, become yet another sensational tale of the brutal exploitation of a young, innocent, helpless slave girl. Given the indisputable facts of the case, unless delicately directed the trial might lead to the charge that the southern legal structure ignored the humanity of the slave and condoned such sexual abuse and exploitation. Indeed, the *Liberator*, William Lloyd Garrison's paper, did carry an account of Newsom's death at Celia's hands. Ironically, and fortunately for Hall, the *Liberator*'s account was penned by a local correspondent who accepted the early reports of Newsom's death, and repeated the supposition that Celia had acted without motive. Significantly, the *Liberator* reported the story in an occasional feature entitled "Catalogue of Southern Crimes and Horrors."[2] Had the *Liberator* known of the motive for Celia's actions, her trial almost certainly would have received more attention from that paper. Had that happened, because the abolitionist press followed the standard journalistic practice of reporting items gleaned from other papers, Celia's story would have received attention in even more abolitionist papers.

In addition to having to consider how slavery's foes might possibly employ Celia's trial in their behalf, Judge Hall also had to determine to what extent it presented him with a potential political dilemma. Proslavery Missourians would expect to see Celia hang; those less supportive of the institution would expect the court to treat her fairly, or at least in accordance with the law. His political experience, and the fact that his central Missouri constituency contained both Benton and Atchinson supporters, no doubt alerted Hall to the possible political implications of Celia's trial. Given the impact of the slavery issue upon Missouri's politics at the time, he probably hoped for the trial to be conducted as expeditiously and decorously as possible, in a manner that ran the least risk of arousing the ire of either camp.

If these considerations weighed upon Circuit Court Judge William Hall as the court's fall term approached, he could have made no more appropriate choice of defense attorney for Celia than John Jameson. Hall needed a capable attorney, one of considerable standing in the community. He needed an attorney with proven political sensibilities, one who had not participated significantly in the slavery debates. In short, he needed an attorney who could be depended upon to give Celia a credible defense, one whose presence would make it difficult for slavery's critics to label the trial a farce or sham, and one who would not arouse the emotions of Missouri's more militant proslavery faction in the process. Measured against these criteria, John Jameson emerged as the superior candidate for the assignment of defending Celia.

Jameson occupied a unique position in Fulton and Callaway County at the time of Celia's trial. The record indicates that although he was a respected figure, he remained a public personage of Falstaffian overtones. For more than three decades he had been a community leader, yet his accomplishments appear to be those of the likable man, the hail-fellow-well-met, rather than those of the truly exceptional individual. There was a discernible gap between his aspirations and his accomplishments, an almost comic aspect to his career that bespoke not so much ineptitude but rather a lack of ambition, a complacency indicative of a ready willingness to be satisfied with comforts and honors easily obtained.

This pattern emerged early in Jameson's career and at times seemed determined by circumstances beyond his control. For example, soon after his first term in the Missouri legislature the Black Hawk War presented Jameson with an opportunity to enhance his political fortunes through military service. As a captain in the militia he led one of two area companies during the hostilities. Jameson's company departed Fulton on July 1, 1832, for a six-week tour of duty. The company spent the entire tour stationed at Fort Pike on the Des Moines River and never engaged the enemy, thus depriving Jameson of the opportunity to earn the politically desirable label of Indian fighter. Other lost opportunities, however, resulted more directly from Jameson's personal failings. As a legislator in the Missouri House, Jameson was not noted for his originality. More significant, perhaps, was his reputation for failing to master the details of legislative service. He was, in the opinion of his contemporaries, "by no means a thorough parliamentarian." His elevation to the speakership, which he occupied for the 1834–36 term, reflected the judgment of members of both parties that, though Jameson might not be among the body's keenest intellects or its most diligent students of the legislative process, he was nevertheless a fair man, one of "judgement and integrity." Competent, likable, and not overly ambitious, he was the perfect compromise candidate.[3]

Jameson's congressional service did nothing to reverse his reputation as an affable, competent man. People of Callaway County judged his congressional career as "in no sense brilliant," noting, however, that "he made a fair member, and proved a strong advocate of Western interests." His congressional record confirms that judgment. He was responsible for no major legislation and in floor debates championed efforts to strengthen the army's ability to control potential Indian threats to western settlers, an echo of his experience in the Black Hawk War. An ardent expansionist, Jameson vigorously defended President James K. Polk's foreign policy and the resulting war with Mexico. Yet he always couched his support in patriotic terms, without any defense of slavery or appeals for continued opportunities for the institution to expand. In one of his most notable speeches on the House floor—a biting, sarcastic attack—he ridiculed the young Illinois Whig representative Abraham Lincoln for his "Spot Resolution" and his continued opposition to the war, noting that Whig "patriots" from Lincoln's district had fought and died at Buena Vista. His support of the Mexican War resulted in Benton bitterly denouncing Jameson in 1849. The acrimonious debates over Mexico within Missouri's Democratic party between Benton and anti-Benton forces may have contributed to Jameson's decision not to stand for reelection in 1848. Jameson's congressional career was appropriately summarized in an assessment rendered by Callaway citizens within thirty years of his death: "Captain Jameson exercised considerable influence in Congress by his pleasant and affable demeanor, and by the good, practical sense which he exhibited on all occasions;

but his want of application and study prevented him from obtaining a national reputation."[4]

Jameson's legal accomplishments and reputation closely paralleled his political achievements, for similar reasons. According to those who knew him: "As a lawyer he was not profound." Jameson's lack of profundity, at least in part, resulted from his "reluctance to labor and research" which "made it necessary for him to have a law partner." Although he was clearly no legal scholar, Jameson's contemporaries nevertheless admired him for his courtroom skills. "As a jury advocate," they judged, "he was not excelled by anyone in central Missouri, and by few, if any, in the State." His powers as a trial lawyer resulted in part from his ability to present his case forcefully and dramatically, and in part from a flair for the cross-examination of opposing witnesses. His greatest gift as a courtroom performer, however, lay not in his presentation skills, but in his almost uncanny ability to read a jury. "He was," again according to some who knew him, "an excellent judge of men, and seemed to divine, almost at a glance, what particular line of argument would reach and influence each juror; in fact, he could almost read by intuition the thoughts of each juror on the panel."[5]

More than an aversion to work, however pronounced, contributed to Jameson's failure to achieve a national reputation in either politics or law, or to become a significant figure in Missouri's political and legal circles. By all accounts Jameson was a genial fellow who enjoyed the male camaraderie of antebellum politics, an essential element of which was an indulgence in a variety of alcoholic beverages. He was evidently a willing participant in such rituals and throughout much of his political career, if not afterwards, evidenced a fondness for distilled spirits that eroded his professional and political reputation. On occasions "he would imbibe a little too freely, producing a slight unsteadiness in his walk, which he seemed to apprehend would be noticed." Jameson fully understood the social behavior and value systems of his male constituents, however, and possessed the grace and wit to devise an acceptable, if rather transparent, excuse for his occasional stagger. To avert questions about his balance, Jameson would tie a silk handkerchief about his knee and complain of rheumatism. Should his complaints elicit an expression of sympathy, Jameson would reply: "It is immaterial." Jameson employed this tactic frequently enough to acquire for himself the sobriquet "Immaterial John."[6]

William Hall's choice of John Jameson as Celia's court-appointed defense attorney seemed a savvy political move, if not a stroke of genius. Critics could not charge that Celia had been denied adequate representation. Jameson had practiced law in the community for three decades and had a reputation as an excellent trial lawyer. He was a respected citizen, a successful man, a three-term member of Congress, former speaker of the Missouri state legislature. He had never become involved in the heated slavery debates, not even as a member of Congress at a time which presented ample opportunity to do so. Nor had he, so far as the record indicates, become involved in the past summer's rancorous debates over slavery within Missouri. He was himself a slaveowner, yet there is no record to indicate that he was anything other than the "good" master, a proposition that his recent interest in the ministry would support. Nor is there any indication that he was a fire-eating southerner, determined to see the spread of slavery into the western territories regardless of the consequences to the Union. While he had acquired a reputation as a bit of a tippler during his active political career, there is no evidence that alcohol abuse rendered him incompetent, or, for that matter, that he had continued drinking after leaving politics. In fact, there seemed to be every reason for Judge Hall to suppose that John Jameson would give Celia a good, sound, if predictable and unimaginative, defense.

Hall's actions also indicate that the judge was well aware of Jameson's potential liabilities, especially his aversion to legal research, and that the judge went to some lengths to counter them. Although he was not compelled to do so, Judge Hall appointed two attorneys to aid Jameson with Celia's defense. Whether he did so at Jameson's request or of his own accord, we do not know. The fact that be made the appointments, however, again underscores the probability that Hall wished the trial procedures to be perceived as correct and fair, insofar as the laws of Missouri allowed.

The two additional attorneys appointed were clearly subordinate to Jameson. Neither possessed outstanding legal credentials, although both would have appeared to their contemporaries as thoroughly competent. The two possessed strikingly similar family backgrounds and professional credentials. Nathan Chapman Kouns was twenty-two years of age in 1855, the son of one of Fulton's most prominent citizens. His father, Nathan Kouns, had moved from Virginia to Missouri, and in 1855 was the town's most respected physician. Like Robert Newsom and John Jameson, the elder Kouns had prospered in Callaway County; in 1850 he owned real estate valued at $7,000. By that date Kouns also had acquired four slaves, two females, ages twenty-three and eighteen, and two children, a girl seven and a boy two. Active in community affairs, he was a founding member of Fulton's Masonic lodge. He was married and had five children: four boys and a daughter named Margaret, who was twenty-three years old at the time of the trial, roughly the age of Celia and her father's adult female slaves. Nathan Chapman, the eldest son, was educated at home by tutors, then attended St. Charles College, from which he graduated in 1852. He returned to Fulton where he read law for three years, perhaps under Jameson, although the law office in which he studied is not recorded. He was admitted to the Missouri bar in 1855. Thus, at the time of Celia's trial, Kouns was essentially without trial experience, although better educated than many of his fellow attorneys. In all probability, he continued to live at his father's home.[7]

The second appointee, a bit older and better educated, was hardly more experienced. In 1855 Isaac M. Boulware was a fledgling lawyer, twenty-six years of age, and like Kouns, "a representative of one of the oldest and best families in the county." His father was Theodorick Boulware, who had established Fulton's original Baptist church and the family's reputation, wealth, and social position. A Baptist minister of Irish heritage, Theodorick left his native Virginia for Kentucky, then moved to Callaway County in 1827. The elder Boulware had labored at a frantic pace, farming, teaching school, and ministering to several of the county's Baptist churches. Theodorick's energy and relentless determination to succeed did not go unrewarded. By 1850, when Theodorick was sixty-nine, he had acquired a small fortune—real estate valued at more than $8,000, large herds of livestock, and more than a dozen slaves. He had become the patriarch of one of Callaway County's wealthiest families.[8]

The last of eight children, Isaac was perfectly positioned within the family to take full advantage of his father's hard-won wealth. The young Boulware attended Transylvania University in Lexington, Kentucky, then one of the South's most respected institutions. Upon his graduation Isaac returned to Fulton, where he read law under a Judge Ansell. After this initial legal training he once more journeyed to Lexington, where he enrolled in Transylvania's school of law. He graduated in 1854 and returned to his Fulton home, thus becoming one of the state's few lawyers who held a professional degree. He was admitted to the Missouri bar a year later, within months of his court-ordered assignment to Celia's case. Given the family background and legal training of Boulware and Kouns, it appears obvious that Judge Hall assigned the bright, well-educated, if inexperienced, young lawyers to aid Jameson with the detailed legal research the older man dreaded. Their impeccable family credentials would have blunted potential criticism of their assignment to the case. Though both came from slaveholding families, because of their youth they had not become publicly identified with the slavery controversy. Thus, they seemed perfect candidates for their positions.[9]

Whatever the intent of Judge Hall in assembling this particular array of legal talent to provide Celia's defense, there were two factors in Jameson's life that might have given him pause had his strategy been to obtain a correct, perfunctory trial. The first was Jameson's family. Jameson was the father of three daughters, the oldest of whom, Elizabeth, was fourteen in 1855, while Sarah, the middle girl, was twelve. Hall may well have considered the possibility that Jameson, though himself a slaveholder, as the father of two adolescent girls might develop a certain amount of sympathy for Celia. Jameson's relationship to his daughters may have had no influence upon his attitude toward Celia. Certainly the fact that Robert Newsom was the father of two daughters who resided in his household had not influenced his attitudes about or conduct toward Celia. Nevertheless the circumstances of the case, especially Celia's youth and Newsom's undeniable sexual exploitation of her, increased the possibility that Jameson would develop some empathy toward Celia because of his daughters. The possibility was increased by the second factor, the fact that since his retirement from politics Jameson had become seriously interested in the ministry and had studied for and received ordination in the Christian church. Such a considerable investment of time and effort in religious studies at this late stage of Jameson's career raised the possibility that

Jameson might be inclined to explore seriously the moral implications of the case. That he himself had owned female slaves, and very well may have owned a twenty-one-year-old female slave at the time, would not necessarily have deterred him from doing so. In fact, if Jameson took seriously the owner's moral obligation to treat his slaves well, as did many of the southern clergy who sought to reform the institution they believed God ordained, he may have felt obliged to do so. His serious interest in religion raised the possibility that he might decide to mount something beyond the usual defense on behalf of a client, who, though a slave, appeared to be morally, if not legally, innocent of the crime with which she was charged.[10]

Certainly events within the Disciples of Christ had presented anyone seriously considering entering its ministry with the moral dimension of the slavery issue. The denomination, which had developed from the earlier Campbellite Presbyterian movement of the southwestern frontier, was by 1845 divided into three camps. In the deep South, Disciples saw no moral dilemma in the holding of human chattels, while in the North a small but growing abolitionist faction was increasing its attacks upon the institution. Caught in the middle of this doctrinal warfare were the moderates of the North, especially moderates of the border states of Kentucky and Missouri. The battle had been joined in earnest in 1845 when Disciples leader Alexander Campbell published a series of articles defending slavery in the *Harbinger*, the denomination's journal. The Campbell articles drew an immediate response from abolitionists within the denomination, and by 1854 the more radical element had established its own paper, *North-Western Christian Magazine*. Both abolitionists and supporters of slavery aimed their propaganda at the moderates of the border states, where the church was especially strong. Because of both their strength in numbers and their strategic geographic

position, border state members represented a potentially deci-
sive minority that both abolitionists and proslavery advocates
hoped to convert to their position.

Aware that the slavery issue threatened the continued existence of the national denomination, Campbell, who personally
opposed slavery, sought to defuse the issue. In an effort to
prevent the Disciples from splitting into separate, regional
denominations, as had the Baptists, Methodists, and Presbyterians, Campbell and his supporters sought to weather the
storm by refusing to make slavery an issue of faith, declaring
instead that members were free to hold whatever opinions
about the institution their consciences dictated. Like northern
Democrats with their doctrine of popular sovereignty, and for
much the same reasons, Campbell insisted that slavery was a
political rather than a religious issue. Throughout the growing
denominational crisis, Campbell doggedly maintained that "as
American citizens, the members of our churches have the
same political rights with the members of all communities.
They may become 'Whigs' or 'Democrats,' 'Liberty' or 'Pro-
Slavery men,' according to their views of political expedience
and propriety. On these views we all have our opinions."[11]

Thus in the summer of 1855 nothing in the doctrines of
the Christian church prevented Jameson from defending Celia
aggressively. As an ordained Disciples minister, he would have
been fully aware of the debate over slavery within the church,
and as a former Congressman he would have been fully aware
of the political significance of the slavery question. This was
especially true because of his Missouri residency, for despite
Campbell's effort to defuse the issue, by 1855 border state
members were badly divided over slavery, even more so
than the denomination as a whole. Whatever his personal
feelings about slavery in that summer, Jameson would have
approached Celia's case fully aware of its potential implications
for the manner in which his fellow churchmen and residents of

Callaway County, perhaps all Missourians, regarded slavery.

There is no evidence to indicate Jameson's opinion about the guilt or innocence of Celia before she became his client, although he certainly would have been aware of her deed almost the moment it was committed. In a town the size of Fulton it would have been impossible for members of the legal fraternity to have long remained ignorant of the case. What the evidence discloses is only that Judge Hall appointed Jameson and his assistants as defense counsel on August 16, the same day on which Celia was formally indicted by a grand jury. Because her trial was set for the circuit court's October term, Hall's appointment forced Jameson and his colleagues into the immediate preparation of a defense for their client. Simultaneously, court officials prepared for the circuit court's approaching fall term, including arrangements for Celia's trial. Most of the preparation fell to George Bartey (also spelled Bartley), clerk of the court. The son of a Scotch immigrant, George Bartey moved to Missouri as a young man from his native Virginia. He served as deputy clerk of the court, then as clerk. By late September, Bartey had prepared summonses for the jurors and witnesses for Celia's trial, and they had been delivered by Sheriff William Snell.[12]

On the morning of October 9, 1855, while thousands of antislavery Kansas settlers defied the recently elected proslavery territorial government, Sheriff William Snell delivered Celia to the Callaway County courthouse for trial before the circuit court. For an unlettered slave approximately nineteen years of age who may have been pregnant at the time, the solemn courtroom must have been a terrifying and hostile place. She faced the unavoidable stares of strangers and the family and friends of the man she stood accused of murdering. The courts of the State of Missouri were not of her world. She knew about them only what her lawyers would have told her in preparation for the trial. Although there is no record of such conferences, the defense's detailed knowledge of Celia's circumstances evident in the trial record indicate that they occurred. It is also unlikely that such an experienced trial attorney as Jameson would have entered the courtroom without a thorough personal interrogation of his client.

Whatever their contact with Celia, the defense attorneys were the only persons in the courtroom from whom Celia might expect the slightest sympathy. The twelve-man jury, drawn from Callaway County's white male population, had as its foreman William J. Selby, a forty-six-year-old justice of the peace from Cedar Township. The son of a Methodist preacher from Maryland, Selby arrived in Missouri in 1824. By 1850 he was a successful farmer whose real estate and livestock holdings were worth approximately $3,000.[13] In addition to Judge William Hall and the clerk, George Bartey, court officials present included Sheriff Snell and circuit attorney R. G. Prewitt.

Although the court records refer only to "counsel for the defense," it was Jameson who presented Celia's case to the jury. Given Jameson's reputation as a formidable jury advocate and the youth and inexperience of his colleagues, it is highly improbable that either Boulware or Kouns argued the case. Also, with Jameson presenting the case for the defense to the jury, Prewitt faced several disadvantages. As a resident of Howard County, the next county upriver from Callaway beyond neighboring Boone County, it was unlikely that Prewitt was known personally by members of the jury, whereas Jameson was a well known and respected local figure. Prewitt was also a relatively inexperienced prosecutor, having served as circuit attorney for less than two years.[14]

The jury impaneled and sworn "to try the issue of whether defendant was guilty of the crime of murder charged against her," was, like the inquest jury that had first indicted Celia, typical of the male residents of Callaway County. Their names reflected the essentially British heritage of the county's residents: William J. Selby (foreman), William Givens, Stephen Gilbert, William Lloyd, Benjamin Sheets, Thomas Pratt, John Culbretson, William Craig, W. J. Ficklin, William P. Selby, George Hossman, and Samuel Maties. The members ranged in age from Stephen Gilbert, thirty-four, to William Selby, seventy-five, the foreman's father. Only one, Thomas Pratt, forty-three, was a native of Missouri. Most, seven in all, had been born in Kentucky, then migrated westward, some as adults, some as children. All of the jurors were married, except for the elder Selby, who had lost his wife. All had children; most had large families. In 1850 the younger Selby had six children, whose ages ranged from sixteen to five. Maties had four children: Pratt, three; Craig, four; Culbretson, seven; Sheets, eight; Givens, two; Ficklin, three; and Lloyd, four. In the same year a son, his wife, and two grandchildren resided with the elder Selby. Provided the children of jurors listed in the 1850 census survived in 1855, five of the jurors, including the foreman, would have had daughters approximately Celia's age. Whether this fact reflects the normal pattern of gender distribution in the large families favored by Callaway's residents, or the skill of the defense at jury selection cannot be known. The nature of the defense's presentation, however, suggests that the latter was the case.

The jurors were not particularly prosperous, although three had substantial holdings. None of them owned in 1850 real estate as valuable as that of Newsom. The holdings of William J. Selby, valued at $2,000, and of William Givens, valued at $3,000, were the largest. One juror, Samuel Maties, owned no property in 1850, four others held real estate valued at $500 or less. All were farmers, including the elder Selby, also a Methodist minister. At least four of the men owned slaves: Gilbert, Givens, Sheets, and Craig. Givens, the wealthiest of the twelve, in 1850 appears to have owned a slave family, a male twenty-two and a female twenty-six, and three children, age six and under. William Craig, whose real estate holdings were valued at $1,600, owned fourteen slaves, four adults and ten children. Benjamin Sheets's slave holdings in 1850 resembled those of Newsom, three male adults, one woman, and two children. Stephen Gilbert listed a male slave, fourteen, in 1850. Thus a jury of farmers, all fathers, on the whole less prosperous than Newsom, less than half of whom appear themselves to have been slaveholders, would determine Celia's guilt or innocence. From the perspective of the defense, the jury was about as good as could be expected.[15]

Preliminaries consumed most of the first day. Counsel for the defense pled Celia not guilty to the charge of murdering her late master, Robert Newsom, and announced Celia "ready for trial, and prayed herself upon her God and her Country." Thereafter the court adjourned, Judge Hall sending the jurors home and Celia back to her cell.[16] When on the following morning the trial resumed, the courtroom drama played quickly and predictably. The prosecution called as its first witness Jameson's nephew, Colonel Jefferson Jones. Under questioning from the prosecution Jones related his conversation with Celia after she had been indicted and jailed. He revealed that Celia admitted she "had been having sexual intercourse" with Newsom. Jones also testified that Celia had told him that George had demanded that she have no further sexual relations with their master. He then described the manner in which Celia had killed Newsom and the way in which she disposed of the body. The entirety of his testimony for the prosecution was descriptive, lacking the slightest reference to a possible motive for the crime.

Jameson's cross-examination quickly established a key element of a planned defense that became fully evident only after all testimony had been heard. He immediately focused on the sexual nature of the relationship between Celia and

Newsom, forcing Jones to admit that Celia had told him that Newsom had raped her on the return trip from Audrain County immediately after his purchase of her, that he had continued to demand sexual favors of her throughout the years she resided on the Newsom farm, and that he had fathered her children. Jameson's detailed knowledge of Celia's relationship with Newsom strongly indicates that Celia had confided in her defense counsel, for it is unlikely that the prosecution would have provided him with this information. Evidently uneasy with this line of questioning, Jones responded with tentative answers, attempting to foil Jameson's efforts to portray Newsom as a fiend. To Jameson's question about the rape, Jones replied that he "can't say positively whether Celia said the accused had forced her on the way home" and that he did "not know with certainty whether she told me so." The nature of the colonel's responses imply Jameson's questions, which were not recorded because at this time trial proceedings were summarized rather than recorded verbatim. It is clear, however, that Jameson continued to press him on this issue, attempting, through Jones, to supply a reason for Celia's actions.

Jones's rather weak contention that "he had heard" that Newsom had raped Celia was certainly a response to Jameson's question that if Celia had not told him Newsom raped her, who had. The summarized exchange between Jones and Jameson about the rape implies that Jameson raised the issue based on information supplied to him by Celia. Jones had not mentioned the rape in his testimony for the prosecution, for obvious reasons, and made every effort to minimize its significance without denying that it took place. His contention that he could not "say positively" whether Celia told him of the rape was a transparently convenient lapse of memory. A white lawyer sent by a judge to question a slave woman who had murdered her master would have recalled whether she said her master raped her on the date of her purchase. Jones may not have replied so tentatively in an effort to convict Celia, or to spare the reputation of Robert Newsom, however. He may well have been reluctant to testify about the matter because Newsom's two daughters were present, and he sought to spare their feelings.

In addition to supplying his client a motive, Jameson also sought to obtain some sympathy for Celia, a fact evident from Jones's response to a question that came immediately after his testimony about Newsom's sexual involvement with his slave. The question was obviously about the age of the accused, for Jones answered that she "said she was about nineteen years old at the time we were conversing." With his cross-examination of Jones, Jameson had established the fact of Newsom's continuing sexual relations with the defendant, the fact that she did not willingly consent, and the probability that she had been raped as a fourteen year old. He also pressed Jones on Celia's intent at the time she struck Newsom, forcing him to testify that Celia had told him that she "did not intend to kill, but only to hurt him [Newsom]." This line of questioning brought an objection from the prosecution, which Judge Hall sustained. Jones's response, though legible in the trial record, is lined out in the clerk's original notes, and the response is dropped from the official record, which was compiled after the trial's completion.[17]

The prosecution next called Virginia Waynescot to the stand. Given Jameson's line of questioning in his cross-examination of Jefferson Jones, Newsom's older daughter undoubtedly approached the witness stand with mixed emotions—a desire for revenge and the conviction of her father's killer, combined with concern for the reputation of the deceased, and by extension, of his family. Following the circuit attorney's lead, Virginia related the family's search for the missing father and the details of the searchers' efforts to recover his remains once they discovered his fate. Again, the prosecution asked no questions about why Celia, a trusted servant, would commit such a violent act. And again Jameson returned to theme of motive in his cross-examination. Virginia Waynescot's answers suggest a set of questions about where Newsom slept and where he had been in the home before the murder. Clearly, Jameson sought to establish in the mind of the jury that Newsom often abandoned his bed for Celia's, thus Virginia's response that she "did not notice the [father's] bed. Sister made the bed up." Jameson also again sought to obtain sympathy for his client, forcing Virginia to admit that Celia "took sick in February. Had been sick ever since." Jameson did not, however, directly ask Virginia about her father's sexual relationship with Celia. To have done so would have been a gross violation of the Victorian sexual mores of the period, a fact an experienced jury advocate such as Jameson would have fully appreciated. With female witnesses, implication was sufficient. He would observe the social mores of the community, only to return to more explicit questioning with male witnesses.[18]

Young Coffee Waynescot next appeared for the prosecution. Under the prosecuting attorney's guidance, the adolescent Coffee related to the jury his horrifying story of removing his grandfather's ashes from Celia's cabin. Jameson's cross-examination was brief and once again without direct reference to Newsom's habitual sexual exploitation of Celia. Once more Jameson focused on where Newsom customarily slept in the home and whether he had gone to bed that night. Coffee, who slept in his mother's room, provided little information Jameson could use to build a defense for his client.

The prosecution followed Coffee Waynescot with William Powell, the neighbor who had led the search for the missing Newsom. In a brief statement Powell matter-of-factly related the manner in which Newsom's bones had been located, not once referring to his interrogation of Celia. Jameson put

Powell through a rigorous cross-examination, much as he had done with Jefferson Jones, stressing similar themes. He asked Powell if he knew whether Newsom had slept in his bed on the night of the murder, and Powell replied that he had not examined the bed. He obtained from Powell testimony that Celia had originally denied knowing anything of Newsom's disappearance, that she had confessed only after she was threatened with the loss of her children and hanging. Under Jameson's questioning, Powell admitted that Celia said Newsom habitually forced her to have sexual intercourse and that she had asked other members of the family to make him stop the practice. He also testified that Celia said she had not intended to kill Newsom, only to hurt him in order to make him stop his sexual demands. Jameson also obtained from Powell an admission that Celia maintained that even as she struck Newsom she acted from desperation, with no intent to kill. Powell's testimony, combined with that of the state's other principal male witness, Jefferson Jones, was crucial to Jameson's planned defense.

The state called as its last witnesses two doctors. Both testified that the bones produced by the prosecution were, indeed, those of an adult human. The defense did not bother to cross-examine either witness. After the state introduced into evidence Celia's signed confession, obtained at the scene of the crime on the day after the murder for the coroner's jury, it rested its case.[19]

The defense began its case by calling to the stand Dr. James M. Martin, a prominent Fulton physician and a man of enough standing in the community to have led an 1853 effort to obtain a railroad for the county. That a man of his prominence would testify for the defense—and nothing in the record suggests that he was a hostile witness—indicates that many of Fulton and Callaway County's citizens were sympathetic to Celia. In Martin's case, that sympathy evidently resulted from the belief that even slaves possessed certain elemental human rights, which owners were bound to respect, rather than from any opposition to slavery. In fact, in 1860 Martin owned five slaves, including two women, forty and twenty years of age, and thus was probably a slaveowner at the time of the trial. It is clear that the defense hoped to use Martin to challenge the state's physical evidence in the case, and to create doubt among the jurors that Celia alone and unaided could have carried out the crime of which she stood accused. This seemed a logical and promising line of defense, since Jameson was aware that in the weeks following Celia's arrest some members of the community, as well as the Newsom family, had continued to suspect that Celia was not alone responsible for her master's death.[20]

To accomplish these objectives Jameson put a series of questions to his first witness. Could the body of an adult human be destroyed in a common fireplace within the space of six hours? Although Jameson assigned the briefest possible time span to the destruction of Newsom's body (Celia may have had as much as eight hours in which to dispose of the corpse), he had pinpointed the issue most responsible for doubts that Celia alone had murdered Newsom and disposed of his body. The burning of a human body in a cabin fireplace must have been a difficult, malodorous affair, requiring constant refueling and constant effort to keep the corpse in the flames. How, the question implied, could this have been accomplished in so short a time by a single woman, only nineteen years of age, who was both sick and pregnant?

The question brought an objection from the prosecution, which Judge Hall sustained. Despite the sustained objection, Jameson refused to abandon this promising line of defense. "What would be the time required for a common wood fire to destroy an adult body?" he asked, rephrasing his question in an effort to avoid again being overruled by the judge. Another objection from the prosecution followed, again sustained. Once more Jameson rephrased his question, trying to meet the prosecutor's objections. "What, in your opinion as a 'scientific physician,'" he asked Martin, "would be the time required to destroy an adult human body?" A third objection from the prosecution, also sustained, caused Jameson finally to abandon his effort to counter the state's physical evidence. However, he objected to each of Judge Hall's sustaining opinions and requested that his exceptions be noted, a request the judge denied. This series of objections to the arguments of the defense, all sustained by Judge Hall, strongly imply that the judge was determined to have a brief, procedurally correct trial in which the state would prevail. Counsel for the defense, however, was not cooperating.[21]

Thomas Shoatman then took the stand for the defense. A Fulton resident, he had accompanied Colonel Jefferson Jones when Celia had been questioned in July about the possible involvement of other slaves in the murder. That Shoatman, unlike Jones, who had been the state's lead witness, was called to testify for the defense without any indication that he was a hostile witness once again suggests that some of Callaway County's residents sympathized with the defendant. Jameson attempted to use Shoatman's testimony to establish that Celia feared for her life at the time she killed Newsom. This was a critical point for the defense, for throughout the slaveholding states the law gave a slave the right to use force to repel physical attacks that threatened his or her life. The legal principle that a slave could, in extreme circumstance, resort to the use of deadly force to protect her life was also one that had been upheld in a number of southern state court decisions.[22]

Shoatman testified that Celia said when she first struck Newsom, he fell and then "threw his hand up to catch her." The prosecution objected to the testimony. Again Judge Hall sustained the objection, and the clerk struck from the record the phrase "to catch her." Jameson then reworded his question to the witness as the result of the objection and asked specifically if Celia had said why she struck Newsom the second, and fatal, blow. Shoatman replied that "the reason she gave for striking him the second blow was that he threw up his hands toward her to catch her." Once more the prosecution objected, and Judge Hall sustained the objection. The reference to the threatening nature of Newsom's gesture was stricken from the record. While it is evident from the record that the jury was ordered to disregard this portion of Shoatman's testimony, Jameson had succeeded in presenting to the jury evidence that Celia had acted in self-defense. This accomplished, he queried Shoatman about the reasons Celia gave for first striking Newsom. Shoatman replied she did so without intent to kill Newsom, "only to hurt him, to keep him from having sexual intercourse with her." Again, the prosecution objected to Shoatman's testimony, and the judge ordered that the phrase "to keep him from having sexual intercourse with her" be stricken.[23]

With Shoatman's testimony, Jameson reinforced the themes introduced in his cross-examination of Jones and Powell. Although the judge ordered the jury to disregard Shoatman's testimony that Celia first struck Newsom to prevent him from raping her, Jameson had made sure the jury heard it. Shoatman's testimony also allowed Jameson to implant the idea of self-defense in the minds of the jurors, despite the state's successful objections. He had lived up to his reputation as a skillful jury advocate, presenting the basics of his defense to the jury despite the objections of the prosecution and a presiding judge whose consistent rulings to sustain the state's objections revealed, if not his hostility toward the defendant, at least a desire for a perfunctory defense and a short trial. Jameson also presented the jurors with testimony that Celia had struck the fatal blow in an effort to defend her life. Furthermore, Jameson's willingness to pursue a line of questioning after the state's first sustained objection indicates that his performance was far from perfunctory. The defense was providing Celia the best of their collective abilities in the face of the ill-concealed hostility of the trial judge. Assured that the jury had at least heard the defense's major arguments, Jameson here rested his case. Whatever his motives, his performance revealed that, in this case at least, Jameson believed even a slave accused of her master's murder deserved the best possible defense. Having presented his arguments to the jury, he next attempted to reconcile the essentially moral nature of the case for the defense with the technical constraints of the law. The manner in which he did so suggests that Jameson believed not only that his client deserved the best possible legal defense but that she was morally innocent.

Six

The Verdict

With jury presentations completed Celia's trial entered the stage most crucial to the defense, the determination of jury instructions. Missouri law enabled both the prosecution and defense to request that the judge deliver specific instructions to the jury. It also provided that either side could object to the proposed jury instructions of the other. The judge was at liberty to accept requested instructions either in whole or in part, or he could himself instruct the jury without regard to the requests of either the prosecution or the defense. Thus, the jury's final instructions represented a combination of the instructions requested by the prosecution and the defense, the requested instructions the judge chose to deliver, and instructions not requested which the judge himself decided to issue. Since the instructions delivered had the potential to direct the jury's verdict, it was essential that the defense propose instructions that would provide the jury with a rationale for finding Celia innocent. It was equally essential that the defense develop instructions that Judge Hall would find acceptable and present to the jury.

Because of their significance, jury instructions were carefully drafted. The effectiveness of a set of instructions rested upon a thorough knowledge and understanding of both Missouri's legal statutes and precedent setting court rulings. Jury instructions also afforded attorneys some creativity, an ability to develop original legal concepts and advance arguments never employed in prior cases. Since Jameson admittedly lacked enthusiasm for legal research and was not renowned for his legal creativity, Kouns and the law school graduate Boulware most likely contributed to the strategy of the defense at this stage of the trial.

No matter who developed the strategy, the set of instructions offered by the defense represented a combination of the mundane and the audacious. Among the more predictable of the thirteen separate instructions requested was a statement about presumption of innocence, which drew an objection from the state sustained by Judge Hall. Another three, all eventually given by the judge, requested that the jury return a verdict of not guilty unless it found from the evidence presented that Celia had willfully killed her master, and unless the jury arrived at this conclusion beyond a reasonable doubt. Thus, the instructions the defense requested, like Jameson's cross-examinations of the state's witnesses, placed little emphasis upon disputing whether Celia had, indeed, killed Robert Newsom. The state's overwhelming evidence that she had done so dictated such a strategy by the defense, which never denied that Celia had been responsible for Newsom's death, but focused instead on Celia's motives.

The remainder of the nine instructions requested by the defense dealt with motive. All were designed to provide the jury reasons for acquitting Celia even though the prosecution's evidence proved conclusively that she had struck Newsom a fatal blow. In what was a weak legal argument, the defense requested that Celia be found not guilty of murder in the first degree, the crime with which she was charged, if the jury found that Celia had killed Newsom "without deliberation and premeditation, and in the heat of passion." It also requested that she be found not guilty if the evidence showed "that she did not intend to kill him at the time it was done." These two requested instructions were, in effect, a bid to reduce the charge against Celia to second degree murder and thus spare her life. Though not crucial to the defense, they, too, drew objections from the state, which Judge Hall sustained.[1]

The remaining six requested instructions contained the heart of the defense's case. Each of the six attempted to establish that Celia had the legal right to use force to repel her master's sexual advances. The defense's decision to make this, rather than self-defense, the basis for its case was dictated by Judge Hall's rulings on testimony given during the trial. By sustaining the prosecution's objections to defense questions about Newsom's possible threats against Celia's life, Judge Hall had removed all grounds for a plea of self-defense. The defense had been unable to obtain direct testimony from Celia about a perceived threat upon her life, for under Missouri law, as was the case in most southern states, a slave could not testify against a white person, even one deceased. Judge Hall's refusal to allow any reference to supposed threats on Celia's life, which were all ultimately based on statements made by Celia, was thus technically correct, though it was a severe blow to the defense, for self-defense was the sole legal argument extended by southern courts to slaves accused of capital crimes.[2]

The remaining instructions requested by the defense represented a bold and imaginative response to its inability to plead Celia innocent on grounds of self-defense. Three of the instructions requested specifically called for Celia to be acquitted if the jury found that she had acted to protect herself from an "imminent danger of forced sexual intercourse." One of the three anticipated the jury's possible negative reaction to Celia's having a sexual relationship with both George and Newsom. The defense wanted the jury instructed that prior sexual conduct on Celia's part did not confer upon her master an absolute right to sexual relations with her. "Although the jury may believe from the evidence," the requested instruction read, "that Newsom and another had had sexual intercourse with Celia prior to the time of the said alleged killing, yet if they further believe from the testimony, that the said Newsom at the time of said killing, attempted to compel her against her will to have sexual intercourse with him, they will not find her guilty of murder in the first degree. . . ."

Having presented its argument that, regardless of her past sexual activities, Celia should be acquitted if the jury found from the evidence that she had killed Newsom in an effort to prevent him from having sex with her, the defense proceeded to build its case that Missouri law allowed such a defense. At this point the defense's arguments began to threaten the very foundations of the institution of slavery. Celia, the defense insisted, even though a slave, was entitled by law to use deadly force to protect her honor. Section 29 of the second article of the Missouri statutes of 1845, the legal code in effect at the time of the trial, made it a crime "to take any woman unlawfully against her will and by force, menace or duress, compel her to be defiled." Those convicted of such an act were to be sentenced to three to five years in prison. The defense's requested instructions argued that "the use of a master's authority to compel a slave to be by him defiled is using force, menace and duress, within the meaning of the 29th section of the 2nd article of the Missouri Statutes for 1845." Finally, the defense requested that the jury be instructed that "the words 'any woman' in the first clause of the 29th section of the second article of the laws of Missouri for 1845, concerning crimes and punishments, embrace slave women, as well as free white women."[3] The contention that the term "any woman" included slave women was crucial for the defense, for, according to Missouri law, even first degree murder was justifiable if committed in resisting a person attempting to commit a felony upon the resisting individual.[4]

The defense's contention that Newsom's death was justifiable homicide, that even a slave woman could resist unwanted sexual advances with deadly force, and that the sexual demands of even a master could be legitimately resisted by his human property was as bold as it was brilliant. It certainly was not the jury instructions that would have been expected from competent defense counsel selected to provide a merely adequate defense. With its claim that Celia had the legal right to protect her honor, defense counsel raised a multitude of legal questions about ownership of the reproductive capabilities of a female slave. If, for example, a slave could resist her master's advances, had she also the right to refuse a male partner her master selected for her? The issue of who controlled sexual access to female slaves held tremendous economic, as well as social, significance, for the reproductive capabilities of female slaves were clearly viewed by slaveholders as an economic asset over which they had control.[5] This innovative and daring strategy indicated that counsel for the defense was determined to employ every conceivable legal argument and device to see Celia acquitted.

The prosecution objected to each of the defense's requested instructions employing the justifiable homicide argument, forcing Judge William Hall to choose between the instructions proposed by the defense and those proposed by the state. The prosecution's requested instructions which, like its case, simply ignored motive, claimed instead that "the defendant had no right to kill [Newsom] because he came to her cabin and was talking to her about having intercourse with her or any thing else." In yet another of the prosecution's suggested instructions, the contention was put more forcefully: "If Newsom was in the habit of having intercourse with the defendant who was his slave and went to her cabin on the night he was killed to have intercourse with her or for any other purpose," Celia had no right to take his life and should be convicted. Finally, the prosecution requested that the jury be instructed that "there is no evidence before the jury that [Celia] was acting in self defense." The jury was to consider neither the defendant's motives nor her intentions. If the jury determined that the evidence and testimony presented proved that Celia, for any reason, had killed Newsom as charged, it was to return a verdict of guilty.[6] Thus the instructions requested by the prosecution, were, in effect, a recognition of a master's right to demand sexual favors of his slaves.

The defense objected to each of the prosecution's proposed instructions, with one exception, a statement to the jury that it was to convict Celia unless the evidence showed "to the reasonable satisfaction of the jury that she was guilty of a lesser crime or acted in self defense." The inclusion of this item in the instructions requested by the prosecution was merely an acknowledgment that the law allowed a slave to protect her life, even against threats from a master. However, the prosecution had also specifically requested that the jury be instructed to find that no evidence indicated that Celia's life was threatened by Newsom. Since the prosecution objected to the crucial instructions requested by the defense, and the defense objected to requested instructions central to the prosecution's position, it fell to Judge William Hall to decide which instructions would be given. On his decision rested Celia's fate.[7]

Because of the tenacity and creativity of the defense counsel he had appointed, Judge William Hall now faced a personal choice with inescapable moral implications. Whether the moral implications of the decision he faced troubled him is impossible to know. That he understood the moral implications of his decision, however, seems evident, for the simple reason that Celia's counsel chose to advance an essentially moral defense. Whether he found the choice easy or difficult, the judge came down squarely on the side of the prosecution. Over the objections and exceptions of the defense, which again indicated how seriously the defense approached this case, he delivered to the jury every instruction requested by the prosecution. He also sustained the prosecution's objections to all but three of the instructions requested by the defense, once again over the objections and exceptions of defense counsel. None of the three defense instructions the judge delivered to the jury introduced the central issue of motive. Rather, the defense instructions Hall read to the jury dealt with the technicalities of reasonable doubt and the weight to be given Celia's confession.[8]

Judge Hall's denial of the defense's instructions to acquit Celia because of Newsom's sexual assault was practically a foregone conclusion. The trial testimony of both prosecution and defense witnesses established beyond dispute that Newsom had been in the habit of demanding sexual favors of Celia, and that she had resisted those demands over a period of several months. Testimony from both state and defense witnesses also established beyond reasonable doubt that Newsom went to Celia's cabin on the night of his death with the intention of again forcing her to have intercourse with him. Yet the defense's contention that a slave woman had the right to use force to prevent rape, especially rape by her master, was highly novel. In Missouri, sexual assault on a slave woman by white males was considered trespass, not rape, and an owner could hardly be charged with trespassing upon his own property. Missouri's failure to make the rape of a slave a crime was hardly unique. Rather, throughout the antebellum South, as historians from Ulrich Phillips to Eugene Genovese have observed, the law did not recognize the rape of black women. As Genovese has bluntly put it: "Rape meant, by definition, rape of white women, for no such crime as rape of a black woman existed at law."[9]

It was not narrow legal technicalities, however, that most threatened the acceptance of the defense's requested instructions. The defense's contention that slave women had a legal right to protect their honor, that the term "any woman" in Missouri's general statutes applied to slaves was a truly radical notion, threatening both a fundamental concept of slave law and the everyday operations of slavery. According to a recent study of slave law in the American South, one of its "two primary characteristics" was "the effort, repeated in various forms, to confine the content of slave law to the situation of the slave alone." The law was used in an effort to categorize, to divide the society into two components, one slave and black, the other white and free. It was a system that ultimately failed, not from a lack of effort to enforce it by southern courts, but because of the nature of human property and the additional burden the very existence of a population of free blacks placed upon the system. Celia's defense attorneys requested not only that Judge Hall abandon any effort to confine slave law to slaves, but also that he extend the protection of the general statutes to Missouri's slave population, in effect nullifying the underlying concept of slave codes.[10]

This contention by the defense was a much more radical concept than that advanced by the attorneys for Dred Scott, whose celebrated case was even then winding its way through the courts. At least from the perspective of the State of Missouri, the central issue in the Scott case was that of comity. Scott based his claim to freedom on residency in a free state. In the past, Missouri courts had ruled that masters who took slaves into free states or territories thereby emancipated them. By the 1850s, however, the Missouri Supreme Court had become more sympathetic to slaveowners, and the court decided in 1852 that Scott remained a slave. The court's ruling rested primarily on the concept of comity. "Every state," wrote Judge William Scott, "has the right of determining how far, in a spirit of comity, it will respect the laws of other states." The amount of respect granted the laws of other states, he continued, would depend upon "their conformity to the policy of our institutions." In a statement that starkly revealed the Missouri Supreme Court's increasingly proslavery sentiments, Judge Scott proclaimed: "No State is bound to carry into effect enactments [of another state] conceived in a spirit hostile to that which pervades her own laws." The United States Supreme Court eventually upheld this view in its famed ruling of 1857.[11]

Although the Missouri Supreme Court's ruling in *Scott v. Emerson* in 1852 underscored the court's proslavery sentiments, given the nature of the legal arguments involved, a contrary finding would have had little effect upon the institution of slavery in Missouri. Indeed, until the 1850s Missouri courts had consistently ruled that masters who took their slaves into free states or territories risked losing their property. Such was the case, a court held in 1836 in *Rachel v. Walker*, even for military personnel who carried slaves with them to posts in free states. While military assignments were mandatory, the court had ruled, the decision to transport a personal slave into a free state was a purely voluntary one. Although the results of the *Scott* and *Rachel* cases were contradictory, the legal position of the court had remained the same. The State of Missouri determined to what degree it would recognize the laws of other states.[12]

Had the Missouri Supreme Court in 1852 seen fit to free Dred Scott, that decision would have had little impact on the routine operations of the institution of slavery within the state.

112

Some slaveholders might have weighed more seriously the risk of taking their slaves on trips into free states. Given the rising antislavery sentiments in many parts of the North, a few might have canceled travel plans. But within Missouri the nature and operations of the institution would have remained unchanged. The authority of masters over their slaves would not have been threatened, nor would any additional legal protection or privilege have been extended to those in bondage.

The arguments advanced by the defense in Celia's case, on the other hand, posed an immediate threat, one of enormous magnitude to slaveholders. Had it been accepted, not only would it have struck a devastating blow to the authority of slaveowners, it also would have challenged one of the fundamental, if unspoken, premises of a patriarchal slaveholding society. The sexual politics of slavery presented an exact paradigm of the power relationships within the larger society.[13] Black female slaves were essentially powerless in a slave society, unable to legally protect themselves from the physical assaults of either white or black males. White males, at the opposite extreme, were all powerful, with practically unlimited access to black females. The sexual politics of slavery in the antebellum South are perhaps most clearly revealed by the fact that recorded cases of rape of female slaves are virtually nonexistent. Black males were forbidden access to white females, and those charged with raping white females were either executed, or, as in Missouri, castrated, and sometimes lynched. Although on occasion a male slave was charged with raping a female slave, such cases were extremely rare, and convictions even rarer. Indeed, conviction was impossible since slave women were not protected from rape by law, no matter the color of her attacker. In Mississippi, for example, the state supreme court ruled in 1859 that the common law did not protect slaves, and that since no statute made slave rape a crime, a male slave so charged must be released.[14]

While male slaves seldom were charged with raping female slaves, criminal charges against white men for raping slaves simply were not lodged in the antebellum South. A search of Helen Caterall's compendium of slave cases of the American South reveals not a single case in which a white male was charged with raping a slave. While acknowledging that slave women were used by masters for sexual favors, state studies of slavery, including Missouri's, fail to record charges against whites for rape of a female slave. Of course, the lack of such charges merely reflects that the law provided no protection to slave women against rape. If the courts would not convict black males of raping slaves, then such a charge against a white male was ludicrous. Thus, in the antebellum South the rape of slave women by white men, if not expected, was condoned by the law or, more precisely, by the lack of it.[15]

Significantly, the reasons put forward to explain this failing are less than convincing and underscore the significance of Jameson's defense strategy. The law failed to do so, historian Philip Schwarz contends, because to be efficacious, a law against the rape of female slaves by white men meant that the slave would have to testify. Allowing such testimony was unthinkable for white Virginians, the author claims, noting that Virginia judges even refused to hear cases "against any white man for violating common law when the victim was a slave." This questionable assumption avoids the possibility that the rape of slave women could have been made a criminal act, if only to discourage the practice, and assumes that convictions could only be obtained upon the direct testimony of the victim. Indeed, it could be argued that such legislation would have protected the slaveholders' female slaves from potential harm or injury inflicted by a rape committed by a white man. Such legislation also could have been offered in evidence of the masters' concern for the well-being and safety of their slaves. The absence of laws punishing any white men for raping slave women, since such legislation easily could have been framed so as to exclude masters, indicates that far more than the fear of slave testimony lay behind the failure of southern states to pass such legislation.[16] Rather, such legislation was never passed because it would have threatened the master's absolute power over his female slaves.

In an ironic twist, Schwarz's Study, while acknowledging the vulnerability of slave women to sexual assault by white men, sees the lack of criminal penalties for such acts primarily as a deterrent to masters who "would or could have ever taken the slightest legal—and therefore socially effective and significant—action to defend enslaved women against sexual assault by other white men." In other words, since no law made slave rape by white men a crime, it was impossible for whites so inclined to press charges for the rape of a slave. In yet another ironic twist, this same study states that "the almost complete inability of all female slaves to prevent being raped by white men had some influence on the conviction of slaves for rape of white women." The white women that black men raped, the work contends, were not women of position and wealth, nor were they women in male-headed households. They were instead, like slave women, those white women in the society who were basically unprotected and powerless. Thus even from the perspective of some recent scholars, slave women as victims of rape are seen as essentially insignificant, which was precisely the problem that John Jameson and the defense faced in their efforts to save Celia's life in a Missouri courtroom in 1855.[17]

While the lack of criminal cases against white men charged with raping female slaves is an inevitable result of the fact that such rapes were not considered crimes, this void in the criminal record hardly means that such rapes did not occur. The literature on slavery makes it abundantly clear that white men regularly abused female slaves sexually, indeed, deemed sexual access their right. Sexual abuse of female slaves was a prominent theme in abolitionist propaganda precisely because it was an emotionally explosive charge that slavery's foes could document. Slave narratives, by both men and women, were filled with references to sexual demands placed upon female slaves.[18] Planters frequently warned their overseers about clandestine relationships with slave women, for planters were acutely aware of the tendency of overseers to use their power to demand sexual favors and of the potential problems such actions could provoke.[19] The oral histories obtained from former slaves by interviewers employed by the Works Progress Administration during the New Deal contain frequent enough references to the sexual abuse of slave women to indicate that it was not, as southerners claimed, an infrequent occurrence, engaged in only by members of the lower class. The continuing significance of the issue of sexual abuse is evident in the works of some recent historians of slavery. Although the subject is no longer ignored by men, it is explored most effectively in the work of women scholars, one of whom estimates that as many as one in five female slaves experienced sexual exploitation. It also remains a common theme in the works of black creative writers, male and female, a haunting theme of tremendous emotional power, expressed sometimes as sorrow, sometimes as rage. Indeed, since the civil rights movement of the sixties, the sexual abuse of black women by white males has emerged as one of the dominant themes in the works of historians, sociologists, and creative writers.[20]

The sexual vulnerability of female slaves, however, was not simply a metaphor that forcefully conveyed the power of slaveholding men. It was a reality of life under slavery, a feature of the routine operations of a system that regarded humans as property to be used for whatever purpose their owners might wish. It was also a practice that held the potential for economic gain for the master who abused his slave, because the children produced by such unions also became the property of the father. Nor is it accidental that white women were among the most vocal southern critics of the practice. White male access to slave women both threatened the stability of the white family and emphasized the fact that in many respects married white women were little more than the property of their husbands. Even when operating within the private sphere assigned to them by southern society, according to a recent study, white women "belonged within families and households under the governance and protection of their men."[21] In fact, one of the essential legal differences between slave and free women was that free women were protected from sexual assault by law. Although once married white women had no legal recourse against unwanted advances from their husbands, they remained protected from other men.

Acceptance of the defense's argument that slave women were protected by law from sexual exploitation by white men, including their masters, would have granted slave women legal equality with white women in an area of social activity that, more than any other, symbolized class relationships within the South's slaveholding society. In one sense it would have given more protection to slave than to free women, because it would have allowed slave women the right to resist the sexual advances of any man, including masters and husbands, since slave marriages were not afforded legal status. It would have checked the master's absolute power over female slaves to some degree, perhaps not so much as the fear of physical attack by a black mate, but certainly more than fear of social opprobrium. Since slaves could not testify against whites, it would have encouraged slave women, such as Celia, to seek aid from sympathetic whites, aid that could be provided within the law. It would have recognized the humanity of the slave, granted slaves not just a right to life, which the law recognized,

117

but a right to human dignity. White southerners sought to deny slaves precisely this prerogative because of the moral dilemmas inherent within the system. Although the slaves' humanity could never be completely denied, it had to be minimized for the institution of slavery to function. It was in an effort to deny slaves dignity, to deny their humanity, that the law sought to categorize, to define slaves as something other than human, a separate category of being. To have done otherwise, to have recognized by law the basic humanity of slaves, would have created even greater tensions within the society and posed additional moral dilemmas.

The arguments of the defense threatened not only the social assumptions under which slavery operated but the economics of slavery as well. The fertility of slave women was of obvious economic value, since their offspring became assets of the mother's master. Although scholars contend over the degree to which owners interfered in the sex lives of their slaves to insure high fertility rates, that masters were concerned with fertility rates is beyond dispute. By granting slave women the legal right to use force to repel unwanted sexual advances, the defense's instructions would have interfered to some degree with what owners saw as a property right. Such instructions, for example, would have prohibited an owner from arranging marriages between slaves on a plantation, a practice common in the slaveholding states. They inevitably would have had a direct impact upon the economics of slave fertility, one detrimental to the economic interest of slaveholders.

Perhaps most significant, the defense's instructions challenged the role of the white man as the protector of women within southern society. Indeed, it was the duty of the white man to protect all of those in his charge, especially white women. Another generally held expectation within the society was that the slaveholder be responsible for and behave morally toward his human property. While the southern male slaveholder was not a patriarch in the Roman sense, holding the power of life or death over slaves and family members, he was clearly a paternalistic figure, one responsible for those in his family, with slaves seen as part of an extended household. The planter patriarch faced few legal restrictions of his power. Those that existed were difficult to enforce, and thus seldom were. Instead, the society trusted a code of personal honor to restrain the power of the male head of household. Men were to act honorably toward those in their charge and toward those in the charge of other men. The defense's instructions challenged the southern concept of male honor, a crucial element of the South's social system. If slaves could not rely on the protection of their masters, could masters be trusted to protect others in their charge? Specifically, the requested instructions posed the question that if slave women could not be trusted to the protection of their white male masters, and in fact required the protection of the law against their masters, did not white women stand in essentially the same relationship to their husbands?[22]

Thus, the jury instructions requested by the defense threatened some elemental assumptions within southern society. These threatened assumptions were essential both to the routine operations of slavery and to the intellectual defense of the institution that southerners had constructed. They were also essential to the slaveholders' economic interest in the sexual activity of their slaves, and even to the relationship between white men and women. Because of the serious potential threats they posed to slavery, and to that society's essentially patriarchal organization, it was inevitable that Judge William Hall would sustain the state's objections and refuse to deliver them to the jury.

The instructions that Judge Hall delivered to the jury rendered irrelevant any personal doubts about Celia's guilt that individual jurors might have held because of moral or ethical considerations. Denied the ability to acquit on grounds of self-defense, or to find that Celia was justified in using force to repel her master's sexual demands, the jury had no choice but to arrive at one verdict. William Hall's instructions negated Jameson's courtroom presentation skills, and the jury returned a guilty verdict. Judge Hall then remanded Celia to jail to await sentencing.[23]

On the following day, October 11, Celia's three attorneys appeared in court on her behalf and moved "the court to set aside the verdict of the jury . . . and grant a new trial." The defense justified its motion for a new trial on several grounds, all highly critical of Judge Hall's conducting of the trial. The court, according to defense motions, had allowed illegal and incompetent testimony on behalf of the state, excluded legal defense testimony from the jury, refused crucial jury instructions requested by the defense, allowed illegal instructions on behalf of the state, and "refused to give the jury legal instructions as to the law of the case prayed for by the defendant." Judge Hall's rulings, according to the defense, resulted in a verdict that was "against the weight of the evidence, and contrary to the law and evidence," and thus a verdict that was "defective, irregular and informal."[24]

For reasons not indicated in the trial record, Judge Hall did not rule immediately on the defense's request for a new trial, nor did he sentence Celia. Instead there was a delay of one day in both sentencing and ruling on the retrial motion. Perhaps the delay was used to confer with the defense attorneys, or to gauge the political implications of his actions, especially since slavery continued to be a topic of public concern because of continuing events in Kansas. It is also possible that the delay had nothing to do with Celia's trial. Whatever his reason, Judge Hall waited until October 13 to pronounce sentence upon Celia, sentencing her to be "hanged by the neck until dead on the sixteenth day of November 1855." Judge Hall also ordered that Celia "be remanded to jail and kept in close confinement until her execution." Judge Hall then overruled the defense's motion for a retrial, a decision to which the "defendant objected and excepted." The defense immediately countered by requesting an appeal to the Missouri Supreme Court, which was granted.[25]

Tried, convicted, and sentenced to death, Celia was returned to her cell to await her execution. Pregnancy would have delayed Celia's execution date, for under Missouri law a pregnant woman could not be executed, but it is not certain that Celia was pregnant at the time of the trial. The testimony indicates that she was not, for Jameson specifically questioned William Powell about her appearance that June, just after she had killed Newsom. Powell replied that at the time he questioned Celia he did not know that she was pregnant, but that he judged from her appearance that she was. Powell's testimony indicates that Celia was not pregnant at the time of the trial. Also, the trial testimony of Virginia Waynescot fixed February as the date Celia "took sick." Assuming that sickness resulted from her third pregnancy, she must have conceived sometime in January. If this was the case, even if she were pregnant at the time of the trial she should have delivered by mid-November, the date set for her execution. The relationship of her pregnancy to the date of her execution becomes a moot point, however, for some time during her incarceration, whether before or after her trial is not recorded, Celia delivered a stillborn infant while attended by a Dr. Cotten, whose fee the court paid.[26]

Delivered of her dead child, the condemned Celia could only hope that the Missouri Supreme Court would intervene on her behalf. Yet the possibility existed that she would be executed before the supreme court could hear her appeal. According to Missouri law, it was within the trial judge's jurisdiction to issue a stay order to prevent Celia's execution before the supreme court considered her appeal. In a move that must have astonished the defense, Judge Hall refused to issue the requested order for a stay of execution. Evidence presented during the trial perhaps convinced Hall that Celia was deserving of immediate death. It is more likely, however, that once a verdict was rendered the judge wished to dispose of the case as quickly as possible because of political tensions within the state resulting from the ongoing debates over slavery and Kansas. Whatever his reasons, at this juncture in the case of Celia versus Missouri, Judge William Hall again faced a ruling fraught with moral overtones. With his refusal to issue a stay of execution order only the Missouri Supreme Court could intervene on Celia's behalf, and it had to do so before the circuit court's sentence was executed on November 16.[27]

Seven

Final Disposition

The exact nature of Celia's appeal to the Missouri Supreme Court is unknown, for no copy of the appeals document exists. The list of what the defense perceived as irregularities in the conduct of Celia's trial, however, provides a good indication of the language of the appeal. In whatever language the appeal was couched, Judge Hall's failure to issue a stay of execution order rendered it of no avail unless the supreme court acted quickly. As the defense waited for an answer from the supreme court, Celia's execution date drew nearer. By early November it was apparent to Jameson and his colleagues that a very real probability existed that Celia would be executed before the supreme court considered her appeal.

At this juncture, Celia's case took an unexpected turn, one that underscores the moral dilemma her case had thrust upon the people of Fulton and Callaway County. As her date of execution approached, the injustice not only of the trial and its verdict, but also of Hall's refusal to grant a stay of execution, convinced her defense that drastic action must be taken if Celia was to avoid being hanged on November 16.

On the night of November 11, Celia and another black named Matt, also under sentence of death, escaped from the Callaway County jail. Evidence in Celia's file indicates that the escape was planned, that Celia was removed from the jail to prevent her death before a ruling from the supreme court, and that her attorneys, if not involved in her actual escape, were at least aware that she had been freed for that purpose. Writing to the supreme court weeks after Celia's "escape," Jameson, Boulware, and Kouns explained that she did not accomplish her escape unaided. They acknowledged that she "was taken out by some one," although they gave no indication of who that someone might have been. In this extraordinary document, addressed to Abiel Leonard, a circuit court attorney of exceptional ability who had that same year been elected to the supreme court, the three defense attorneys admitted to strong personal feelings about the case. "We feel more than ordinary interest in behalf of the girl Celia," they explained, "believing that she did the act (of slaying Newsom) to prevent a forced sexual assault on the part of Newsom." In a surprisingly blatant effort to bring political pressure, or at least the weight of public opinion, to bear upon the court, the defense also revealed that Celia's case had divided the white community. They informed the supreme court justices that "the greater portion of the community here are much interested in her behalf," clearly implying that the majority of Callaway's citizens opposed Hall's refusal to issue a stay order, if not Celia's conviction.[1]

The defense's admission that Celia was deliberately broken out of jail to prevent her execution before a supreme court ruling is indirectly supported by a newspaper account of the "escape." The press account, gleaned from the columns of the *Fulton Telegraph* and carried by Columbia's *Dollar Missouri*

Journal, notes that Matt, the other slave who escaped, "was returned the next morning," or November 12. Celia, on the other hand, remained at large on November 15, the date on which the report was filed. That Matt "was returned" indicates that he was removed from jail by a party or parties and then purposely and immediately returned by them. The newspaper writer did not say that Matt "was captured," a term that would not have indicated that he was surrendered by a third party.[2] That both Matt and Celia were convicted of murder and yet only Matt "was returned" further suggests that Celia's escape was planned, and that she remained free because certain individuals desired that she do so.

Precisely how long Celia remained at large is not known, but she was not "recaptured," as her defense attorneys explained to the supreme court, until after her original execution date had passed. The evidence in her file strongly suggests that Celia was hidden by those who engineered her escape until after her original execution date had passed, then returned to her captors. This series of events is strongly implied in defense counsel's letter to the supreme court, which states that Celia was "not taken until after the 16th of Nov.," and that the circuit court had set another date, December 21, for her execution. The defense counsel begged the court to examine the record, which they enclosed, expressing satisfaction that the court would find that Judge Hall gave illegal instructions to the jury, while refusing to issue legal ones. The letter concluded with a direct indictment of Hall's judicial conduct, charging that he "indeed cut out all means of defense."[3]

Since defense counsel's letter to Judge Leonard was dated December 6, we know that Celia had been returned to custody sometime between November 16, the original execution date, and December 6. This fact, and the additional information about her "escape" contained in defense counsel's letter to justice Leonard and the newspaper account, strongly suggest the manner in which one group of Fulton and Callaway County citizens, including perhaps one or more of Celia's attorneys, responded to Celia's dilemma and the moral quandary with which her situation presented them. To prevent her execution before every legal means of appeal was exhausted, they conspired to, and did, remove her from the county jail. However, the evidence suggests that Celia's benefactors were not prepared to ignore Missouri law totally, so once her original execution date had passed and it appeared that the supreme court would have an opportunity to hear her appeal, Celia was returned to jail.

There is no indication in the record, either in press accounts or defense counsel's correspondence, that those who aided Celia planned to free her, to see that she reached a free state where she would be immune from further prosecution. The absence of any reference to efforts to remove Celia to free territory presents further circumstantial evidence that one or more of her attorneys were involved in her escape, for such halfway measures would have appealed to lawyers torn between respect for the law and contempt for what they considered Judge Hall's morally inappropriate rulings in Celia's trial. This supposition is further supported by the fact that once Celia was returned to confinement, defense counsel again became concerned that the supreme court act on her appeal before her newly assigned execution date was to arrive. It was this concern that prompted defense counsel's letter to Judge Leonard, in which they urged the supreme court to issue a stay of execution order "until the case can be tried in the Supreme Court in January next." The attorneys implored the court to "please give the matter your earliest attention."[4]

Although the timing of defense counsel's appeal to Judge Leonard was determined by Celia's scheduled date of execution, other factors led them to express their personal concerns about the moral issues raised by the case. Thus it is significant that at the time the appeal was filed Missourians were engaged in yet another period of intense debates over slavery, debates prompted once more by events in Kansas. On October 23, Free Soil party delegates met in Topeka for their constitutional convention, which was presided over by James Lane. Between then and its adjournment on November 11, the convention drafted a constitution that prohibited slavery in Kansas, called for a popular referendum on the status of free blacks in the territory, and scheduled a popular vote on the proposed constitution for December 15. The convention also formally applied to Congress for the admission of Kansas into the Union under the proposed constitution, and created a Free State Executive Committee chaired by Lane and charged with organizing a state government once the proposed constitution was ratified.[5]

The actions of the Topeka convention were widely reported by the Missouri press and drew an instant response from proslavery forces in Missouri and Kansas.[6] Slavery's advocates correctly viewed the Topeka convention as a direct challenge to the authority of Governor Shannon and the territorial legislature. To meet that challenge, on November 14, proslavery representatives met in Leavenworth to form a "Law and Order party." The convention, chaired by Governor Shannon, endorsed the legality of the Shawnee legislature, condemned ex-governor Reeder's election to Congress by the Free Soil party, and passed resolutions warning of civil war should Congress endorse the Topeka constitution and admit Kansas to the Union as a free state. The proslavery *Missouri Republican* saw the Law and Order convention as "well timed and appropriate," although it noted: "There has been too much violence of Language in Kansas on both sides, and trust that the Party of Law and Order will refrain from it." After all, the *Republican* observed, the new Law and Order party was in the right, supporting the duly elected government. The

Kansas correspondent for the antislavery *Daily Democrat*, on the other hand, saw the Law and Order convention as an effort by Shannon to combat a rapid drop in his popularity among the citizens of Kansas. The paper also saw the hand of David Atchinson in these events.[7]

By the end of November, the same time at which Celia was returned to the Callaway County jail to await a new execution date, the mounting tensions between pro- and antislavery forces in Kansas threatened to erupt into a full-fledged civil war. Because of the continuing campaign of Atchinson, Stringfellow, and other Missouri proslavery leaders, it was apparent that an outbreak of violence in Kansas inevitably would result in the active participation of thousands of Missourians. Weapons continued to flow into Kansas as both sides struggled to control the territorial government. The political hostilities and constant ideological warfare finally provoked the threat of mass violence, and for more than a week heavily armed forces from both camps faced one another at Lawrence as politicians from Missouri and Kansas sought to prevent open warfare. This major crisis, in progress at the time Celia's defense counsel wrote urging the supreme court to act on her appeal, received detailed coverage in the Missouri press, and was certainly known to the residents of Callaway County.

The crisis began on November 21, when Celia may have remained at large, since the exact date on which she was returned to custody cannot be determined. It began when proslavery settler Franklin Coleman shot and killed free state settler Charles W. Dow at Hickory Point in Douglas County, near Lawrence, a Free Soil stronghold. Coleman fled to Westport, where he turned himself in to the county sheriff, Samuel Jones. Jones, the acting postmaster of Westport, Missouri, owed his appointment to the proslavery territorial legislature. The following day, Free Soil men gathered in

Hickory Point to protest Dow's shooting, where they met some opposition from proslavery advocates. An altercation occurred, and a proslavery man swore out a warrant for the arrest of one Jacob Branson, with whom Dow had lived. Evidently anticipating trouble, Sheriff Jones arrived in Hickory Point with a fifteen-man posse on November 27 and arrested Branson. On its way to Lecompton, however, the posse was intercepted by a large party of armed free state men and forced to surrender Branson. Jones proceeded to the proslavery town of Franklin, where he wired Governor Shannon that "an open rebellion" had begun in Lawrence, and called for three thousand men with whom to surpress it. Shannon obliged, issuing a proclamation urging the citizens of Kansas to rally to the aid of the sheriff in carrying out the laws enacted by the territorial legislature.[8]

Meanwhile, David Atchinson and his lieutenants began to organize Missouri's border ruffians to rally to the aid of Sheriff Jones and crush the free state rebellion. Rumors of an impending invasion by the ruffians swept through Lawrence, and armed free state men began to pour into the small community from surrounding free state towns. Within days, under the direction of Charles Robinson, James Lane, and General W. P. Richardson, Lawrence was transformed into a fortified garrison. A Missouri reporter described the forces defending Lawrence in the first week of December as composed of four hundred men, among them John Brown and his sons, armed with Sharps rifles, and another four hundred "indifferently armed." "Bold, resolute, and willing to fight," Lawrence's defenders and their two field pieces were entrenched behind "some half dozen earth works" hastily thrown up to repel the rumored attack by the Missouri border ruffians. Under Lane's direction, the men of Lawrence had also appealed to the Congress, the president, and the commandant at Ft. Leavenworth for aid to "quell the riot and prevent further invasion of our peace and security." In an appeal addressed to the people of the nation, the Lawrence defenders charged that a body of troops from a "foreign state," acting directly under the orders of Governor Shannon, threatened to destroy the town and murder its inhabitants.[9]

Outside Lawrence, a proslavery army assembled in two camps, answering Atchinson's call issued December 1 at Platte City, Missouri, urging his fellow Missourians to march on Lawrence to "sustain the Law and put down the Rebellion and Insurrection." Atchinson joined an encampment on Wakarusa Creek of approximately 750 armed men, perhaps more, for reporters favoring free state forces estimated their number at 1,500. Another 700 armed proslavery men were at Lecompton Camp, some three miles to the west. The proslavery forces also possessed at least three cannons, obtained by Clay County, Missouri, ruffians during a raid on the federal arsenal at Liberty. The army of Missourians and their Kansas allies, according to the correspondent of the proslavery *Missouri Republican*, "presents an appearance of daring, bravery, intelligence, high character, and determination which I venture to say was never before seen in the ranks of regulars or militia, in any country, in any age."[10]

Faced with well-armed, determined defenders behind heavily fortified positions, the proslavery forces delayed an attack upon Lawrence, but remained encamped outside the town. The delay allowed for communications between Governor Shannon and leaders of the Free Soil party in Lawrence, and on December 6 Shannon rode from Shawnee Mission to the Wakarusa encampment, where he found the Missourians determined to attack Lawrence, burn the Emigrant Aid Company hotel, and destroy the press of the town's militantly free state paper. Skirmishes on December 7 resulting in casualties on both sides threatened to place events beyond Shannon's control, but a fierce thunderstorm, with hail and high winds, helped cool the ardor of the border ruffians while Shannon and Colonel A. G. Boone of Westport, Missouri, negotiated with representatives of Lane and Robinson.

By the morning of the ninth, the Treaty of Lawrence was agreed upon. The Free Soil men denied any organized resistance to the law and promised to support "proper authority" in the future. Shannon assured the citizens of Lawrence that he had not requested the aid of the border ruffians, and promised to see that the law was enforced without the help of outside forces in the future. The agreement was essentially a face-saving device for both sides, but by preventing violence it avoided the national crisis an attack upon Lawrence almost certainly would have triggered. Even Atchinson and Boone, aware of the political damage to the proslavery cause that might have resulted from an attack on Lawrence, urged the border ruffians to accept the treaty. Despite the grumblings of some hotheads, the proslavery forces, their provisions low and their supplies of whiskey exhausted, decided to accept their leaders' advice and go home.[11]

The Wakarusa War was not the only political crisis fueled by the slavery issue which confronted the people of Missouri and Callaway County in early December, as the recently reimprisoned Celia sat awaiting her newly determined execution date. In the Missouri legislature, which had reconvened in November, Democrats Atchinson and Benton and the Whig Alexander Doniphan had rejoined the senatorial race. At the height of the legislative battle over the contested seat, Atchinson was deeply involved in events in Kansas. On December 1 in Platte City he had delivered a blistering denunciation of the Kansas Free-Soilers, calling upon the men of western Missouri to rush to the aid of Governor Shannon in suppressing Free-Soilers' threats of rebellion and insurrection. Indeed, the fact that Atchinson was in Kansas, attempting to prevent open warfare at Lawrence, a possibility his demagogic oratory had helped create, may have diminished his chances of retaining his Senate seat. Whatever the exact politics of the situation, once again, despite Atchinson's efforts to use his spirited defense of slavery and its expansion into Kansas to retain his Senate seat, no man could obtain a majority. On December 15 the legislature adjourned, leaving the disputed seat vacant.[12]

It was in this heated political atmosphere that the Missouri Supreme Court met in St. Louis for the fall term. The three justices of the court to whom Celia's defense counsel appealed certainly were well apprised of and understood the significance of the slavery issue in their state. They would have been well informed about the bitter Senate race then occurring in Missouri's legislative chambers and the impact of the slavery issue upon the political infighting. They would also have known of the events in Kansas, and of their relationship to the political and social turmoil experienced in recent months by the people of Missouri.

Whether these events influenced the decision of the court's members in the case of Celia can never be determined. All the record reveals is that the three justices, William Scott, John F. Ryland and Abiel Leonard, were fully aware of the facts of the case. They had copies of the trial record, which set forth the testimony of the witnesses and provided copies of all jury instructions requested and given. They also had the personal letter from Celia's defense counsel, which specifically raised the moral issues involved in her case. The performance of Scott and Ryland in the Dred Scott case, however, did not bode well for the appellant. Both had ruled that Scott remained a slave despite his sojourn in free territory. Their decision reversed precedent set by earlier Missouri courts and indicated a decided shift to a proslavery stance by a majority of the court.[13]

Given Jameson's political experience and contacts, it seems likely that Celia's defense counsel knew of Scott and Ryland's

increasingly proslavery inclinations. Perhaps her defense counsel addressed their personal appeal of December 6 to the
recently elected justice Abiel Leonard rather than to his
more experienced colleagues on the Court because they
believed him the most favorably disposed toward their client.
This interpretation is supported by Leonard's political record,
which would have been known by Jameson. A lifelong Whig,
Leonard hoped that both the institution of slavery and the
Union could be preserved. In the late 1840s and early 1850s,
he had attempted to arrange a loose alliance between Unionist
Whigs and Bentonite Democrats to counter the policies and
ambitions of David Atchinson and other proslavery Democrats. In fact, Leonard's efforts contributed substantially to
Atchinson's failure to recapture his Senate seat in 1855.
If Celia's counsel hoped that a more compassionate, more
flexible Leonard could convince his less sympathetic senior
fellows on the bench of the merits of their client's case, of
the need to consider carefully its essentially moral nature, they
hoped in vain.[14]

On December 14, one day before free state voters in
Kansas overwhelmingly endorsed the Topeka constitution,
the Missouri Supreme Court finally ruled on Celia's appeal
and request for the issuance of a stay of execution order. The
court's ruling was brief and to the point. After a paragraph
summary of the nature of the appeal, the ruling announced:
"Upon an examination of the record and proceedings of the
Circuit Court of Callaway County in the above case, it is
thought proper to refuse the prayer of the petitioner:—there
being seen upon inspection of the record aforesaid no probable
cause for such appeal; nor so much doubt as to render it expedi-
ent to take the judgement of the Supreme Court thereon. It is
therefore ordered by the Court, that an order for the stay of
the execution in this case be refused." Whether this was the
opinion of the full court, or that of a majority composed of

Scott and Ryland, is unknown. Perhaps Leonard had argued for Celia, perhaps not. Whatever Leonard's personal stance, it did not save Celia. The court agreed with the trial judge. The moral issues in the case of Celia, a Slave, were judged irrelevant. There was no doubt that she had killed Newsom; the guilty verdict was valid and the death sentence deserved. The court's ruling was received and filed by George Bartey, clerk of the Callaway Circuit Court, on December 18, 1855, three days before Celia's scheduled execution.[15]

With the supreme court's ruling, all appeals were exhausted. Jameson, Boulware, and Kouns lacked any legal means to prevent Celia's execution. This time, no one in Fulton or Callaway County undertook heroic measures to keep Celia from the gallows. Defense counsel, having waged a prolonged and tenacious fight to save Celia, accepted the inevitable, as did those parties unknown who had engineered her "escape" from jail only a month earlier. Whatever Jameson's private thoughts about the impending execution of the nineteen-year-old slave girl, there is no evidence that he, Kouns, or Boulware took further actions to halt Celia's execution. The evidence clearly indicates that Jameson, Kouns, and Boulware saw Celia's conviction and sentence as travesties of justice. Yet neither they nor others in the community who opposed Celia's execution staged a public protest or took additional extralegal measures to save her. This time the sentence of the court would be imposed, the laws of the state of Missouri upheld, the ultimate moral dilemma posed by Celia's case confronted.

During the night of December 20, the eve of her newly designated date of execution, Celia was once again interrogated in her cell. Her interrogators are unknown but probably included officers of the court. Her final interrogation was recorded by a writer for the *Fulton Telegraph*, and once again the issue was whether she had help in the slaying of Robert Newsom.

For the last time Celia denied that "anyone assisted her, or aided or abetted her in any way." She once more related her account of Newsom's death, claiming that she had first struck Newsom without intending to kill him. But, she continued, "as soon as I struck him the Devil got into me, and I struck him with the stick until he was dead, and then rolled him in the fire and burnt him up." This confession on the eve of her execution is probably accurate. Even Celia's insistence that the devil prompted her to strike the blows that killed Newsom seems an apt description of the rage she must have felt on that night. The reporter, however, does not mention Newsom's sexual exploitation of Celia, nor the children that resulted from his abuse.

On the following day, Celia was marched to the gallows. At 2:30 on a Friday afternoon, the trap was sprung and Celia fell to her death. The names of those who participated in or witnessed her death are not recorded, but given the time of execution, it is likely that many of Fulton and Callaway County's citizens stood at the foot of the gallows, One of the witnesses was the unidentified *Telegraph* reporter, in all probability the man who edited the paper throughout the decade of the 1850s, John B. Williams. With unintentional irony, that witness precisely characterized Celia's death: "Thus closed one of the most horrible tragedies ever enacted in our county."[16]

After Celia's death, the Callaway County Circuit Court processed the paper associated with her case, the documents required to see that the cost of administering justice was met. George Bartey, clerk of the court, was paid $14.80 for a variety of tasks, including copying the indictment, issuing subpoenas, swearing in the jury and witnesses, entering an appeal to the supreme court, and completing a record of the case for the supreme court. Sheriff William Snell received $104.50 for summoning witnesses, the expenses of boarding the prisoner, determined at forty cents per day, and for executing Celia's death warrant. D. M. White, justice of the peace, received $2.00 for recording testimony, issuing a subpoena, and taking the oaths of three witnesses. D. S. Whaley was paid $12.00 for providing meals to the jurors, who each received $1.50 for their services. Witnesses at the trial, some of whom were not called to testify, obtained a total of $39.30 for expenses. Robert Prewitt, the prosecuting attorney, earned a fee of $20.00. Celia's trial cost the State of Missouri a grand total of $210.85. On April 18, 1856, Judge William Hall and circuit court attorney Robert Prewitt examined the bill of cash in Celia's case and ordered it "to be certified to the auditor of Public records for payment."[17] The trial record does not reveal the monetary compensation received by counsel for the defense.

Where Celia's remains were interred, much like the events of her life before her fatal confrontation with her master, was not recorded. Just as Celia's final resting place is unknown, there are no records of what became of her children, also the children of Robert Newsom. Although they almost certainly became for a time the property of Newsom's legal heirs, their half brothers and sisters, it is unlikely that they remained with the Newsom family, for their presence would have been a constant and bitter reminder of the events of the summer of 1855. There is, however, the possibility that the nine-year-old female slave Harry Newsom owned in 1860 was Celia's daughter, and his half sister.[18] John Jameson survived Celia by little more than a year. He died suddenly on January 24, 1857, and was buried in the family cemetery in Fulton. Robert Newsom was also interred in a family cemetery, beside his wife, on the farm that they had carved from the Missouri wilderness. His gravestone still stands in a field just off a Callaway County road, some nine miles south of Fulton.

Eight

Conclusions

In a recent essay, historian Darlene Clark Hine observes that "one of the most remarked upon but least analyzed themes in Black women's history" is their "sexual vulnerability and powerlessness as victims of rape and domestic violence." Hine suggests that this theme, so discernible in slave narratives, is accompanied by yet another—"these captive women's efforts to resist the misappropriation and to maintain the integrity of their own sexuality."[1] Although the brief and tragic life of Celia, a slave, cannot provide a comprehensive theory with which to evaluate the manner and degree to which the sexual exploitation of female slaves influenced the routine operations of the institution of slavery, it can and does clearly define the issues that must be analyzed if such a theory is to be developed.

Celia's relationship with Robert Newsom provides a compelling, if hardly unique, example of the power of the white patriarch. Her experience suggests, as does the experience of so many other slave women, that Stanley Elkins's contention that slaves were powerless to protect their most basic humanity from the predations of the master is more accurate than recent scholarship, with its emphasis on agency, cares to admit.[2] In her recent study of plantation women, both slave and free, Elizabeth Fox-Genovese, unlike Elkins, concludes that slave women resisted their masters "in all the ways available to them." Yet the women she describes carried on essentially personal struggles against the practically unlimited power of the master. Slave women could not rely on a fellow slave for protection without placing his life in danger. Nor could they turn to the mistress of the household, who, Fox-Genovese contends, supported slavery. If they lived in a town, as did Harriet Jacobs (whose account of her defense of her virtue is perhaps the best known among slave narratives), they might have obtained support from free blacks or sympathetic whites. But, as Fox-Genovese observes, in 1860 more than half of America's slaves, like Celia, lived on farms with fewer than twenty slaves. Under such conditions it was inevitable that "slave women's resistance was likely to be individual rather than collective." Celia's challenge to her master's power over her sexual integrity was personal, violent, extreme, and unacceptable to a slaveholding society. It was unacceptable because gender mattered in both the social conventions and in the laws that upheld slavery. To have empowered slave women in the domestic arena, to have recognized their right to control their sexuality, would have undercut the power of the master to a degree that would have threatened the very survival of the institution.[3]

Celia's experience also frames the issue of the relationship of slave women to white women in the antebellum South. According to most historians of slavery, considerations of race and class prevented any challenge to patriarchal power by women of both races. Rather, white women chose to support slavery, and to accept, or at least acquiesce to, the abuse of black women it produced. This denial of sisterhood occurred despite the fact that both white and black women were denied their sexual integrity. Married white women were the sexual property of their husbands, with no legal right to refuse their husbands' sexual demands. While Virginia Waynescot and Mary Newsom were not in a marital relationship with Celia's master, they were economically dependent upon their father, just as most farm and plantation wives were economically dependent upon their husbands. Whatever their personal views about slavery, or the abuse of slave women, white women were in no position, legally or economically, to challenge the power of the master effectively. Within such a society, cooperation between black and white women based upon gender-specific issues was a practical impossibility.

The furor over Alice Walker's *The Color Purple* suggests that relationships between black men and women remains an emotionally explosive issue.[4] The basic issues in such relationships are also addressed by Celia's case. Perhaps the most fundamental issue is the extent to which slave men were able to protect the slave women to whom they were attached. Again, the experience of Celia and George, who had no support outside the farm on which they lived, reinforces the bleak assessment of Elkins, and of Fox-Genovese, rather than the more optimistic views of such scholars as Vernon Burton or Stanley Engerman and Robert Fogel.[5] George was unable to prevent Newsom's sexual abuse of Celia, yet he was also unable to deal with it emotionally. It was George's male ego that placed Celia in the quandary that led to Newsom's death and her arrest, conviction, and execution. Yet when faced with a choice between protecting Celia or protecting his own life, George unhesitatingly chose the latter. What the case of Celia documents is the powerlessness of a male slave to protect a loved one, a male slave's smoldering resentment toward his loved one when she was forced into a sexual relationship with her master, and the male slave's natural and understandable act of self-preservation brought about by his equally natural and understandable jealousy. If the conditions that produced the case of Celia were common on the small farms and plantations on which most slaves lived, then tension between black men and women was an inevitable product of slavery.

Celia's case also raises fundamental issues about the role of law in a slave society. Antebellum southerners viewed their slaves as both chattels and persons, a paradox reflected in the legal systems of the slave states. Southern society insisted that the law uphold the master's property rights, while recognizing that as human beings slaves possessed certain rights, including an inviolable right to life. Although historians such as Eugene Genovese have shown that through their responses to the law, slaves, too, helped to shape it, the fact remains that the inevitable conflicts between the recognized human rights of the slaves and the property rights of masters were, with rare exceptions, settled in favor of the masters. It is also true that while the slave codes of the southern states imposed some restrictions on slaveholders, the codes were designed primarily to restrain the behavior of slaves, not their masters.[6]

In his study of slave law, Mark Tushnet contends that one of its major purposes was "to allocate control over slaves to the sentiment of the master class." It could not do so totally, however, for "complete allocation . . . would have removed the regulation of slavery from the sphere of law." Faced with this dilemma, Tushnet suggests, southerners chose to regulate "market transactions" with slave law, leaving "other relationships to be regulated by sentiment." Celia's case demonstrates how difficult an undertaking this was, as long as southerners continued to insist that slaves possessed legal rights. The female slave's lack of a legal protection against rape illustrates the society's preference for sentiment rather than law, but only for women. The sexual activities of black men were not left to sentiment, but rigidly controlled by law, since sexual relations between black men and white women challenged the power of the white man. The law was also used to create the illusion that slaves possessed certain human rights, and thus to assuage the conscience of white society. Procedurally, Celia's trial was correct, yet the substantive, gender-related issues of the case could not be addressed, despite the best efforts of her defense counsel. Thus Celia's trial demonstrates that gender, as well as what Tushnet calls "market transactions," was a significant factor in shaping slave law. Ulrich B. Phillips noted this over seventy years ago when he observed that in the matter of the rape of slave women, "such offences appear to have been left largely to the private cognizance of the masters."[7]

Celia's case also underscores an essential problem faced by those antebellum southerners who hoped to use the law to reform slavery. Such reformers sought to counter abolitionist attacks and make slavery more acceptable to the public of the nonslaveholding states, thus enhancing the institution's chances for survival. Because of the racism that permeated American culture, southern reformers could undertake such efforts with some hope of success. Also, antebellum reformers, especially those with religious backgrounds, genuinely hoped to alleviate slavery's most odious features for humanitarian reasons. Among the reforms most often proposed was recognition of the slave family. Proposals to forbid the sale of slave children and to place slave marriages under the protection of the law were among the most popular. Yet, as Celia's case demonstrates, the nature of slavery in the South would have made the effectiveness of such reforms doubtful, even had such legislation been enacted. So long as slaves remained unable to testify against whites, the owner's power remained virtually unchecked. This was especially the case on farms and plantations, where most southern slaves resided. The physical isolation of the region's farms and plantations made it unlikely that whites other than members of the slaveholding family would witness the abuse of slaves. Yet granting slaves the right to testify against their masters, as opposed to other whites, would have unleashed an avalanche of charges by slaves against their owners, thus compromising the ability of the masters to control their slave labor force. While the sale of slave children could have been halted by legislation, a law recognizing the validity of slave marriages, including the right of female slaves to resist the advances of masters, would have been difficult to enforce without allowing slaves to testify against whites. Such a law, however, might have reduced the incidence of sexual exploitation of slave women by reinforcing the notion that such behavior was socially unacceptable. In any event, such reform legislation was never enacted in the antebellum South, primarily because whites refused to see the states impose any but minor restrictions upon their conduct toward their human property.[8]

Finally, the case of Celia directly addresses one of the central issues in the abolitionist attack upon slavery. Slavery, many of its critics contended, was morally abhorrent, and maintained by slaveholders who, because of their personal knowledge of the institution, understood perfectly well its evils. Slavery was inherently evil, its critics argued, because, as a recent historian notes, it "permitted one group of people unrestrained personal domination over another group of people." Therefore, "the extreme degree of domination required by the system, and not percentages of masters who were cruel or benevolent in their operation of the system, was and is the essential crime."[9] What Celia's case demonstrates is that antebellum southerners, slaveholders and nonslaveholders alike, at some point in their lives were very likely to be confronted with a personal moral dilemma that resulted because slavery granted one group of people such power over another group. These intensely personal decisions, however, as in Celia's case, were made within the context of the larger society and against a backdrop of the continuing debate over slavery. In Missouri, because of the Kansas situation, that debate escalated into political violence at precisely the time at which white Missourians were deciding Celia's fate. The South's retention and spirited defense of the institution suggests that most whites found ways of reconciling slavery, including its denial of the essential humanity of those enslaved, with their personal moral values, as happened in Celia's case.[10] What is unknown, and perhaps ultimately unknowable, is the psychic energy required, both individually and collectively, to facilitate that reconciliation. The events in the last year of Celia's life, although extraordinarily dramatic, demonstrate the nature of the moral choices individuals faced and indicate that some individuals had great difficulty making them. Those events also suggest that the psychic cost to whites of the defense of slavery, though paid, was high, just as they suggest that the psychic cost to blacks, though paid, was incalculable and enduring.

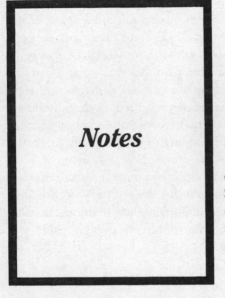

Notes

Introduction

1. Charles G. Sellers, Jr., "The Travail of Slavery," in *The Southerner as American*, ed. Charles G. Sellers, Jr. (Chapel Hill: University of North Carolina Press, 1960), 40–71, especially 69.

2. For an excellent discussion of the moral dilemmas posed by slavery to both nineteenth-century abolitionists and modern historians, see Robert W. Fogel, *Without Consent or Contract: The Rise and Fall of American Slavery* (New York: Norton, 1989), 388–411.

One:
Beginnings

1. *1850 Federal Census for Callaway County, Missouri, Abstract*, compiled by Elizabeth P. Ellsberry, Missouri Depart-

ment of Archives and History, Jefferson City, Mo., 393 (hereinafter cited as *1850 Callaway Census*).

2. Stanley Vestal, *The Missouri* (New York & Toronto: Farrar & Rinehart, 1945), 11–58.

3. *History of Callaway County, Missouri, 1984* (Fulton, Mo.: Kingdom of Callaway Historical Society, 1983), 32–33 (hereinafter cited as *Callaway, 1984); History of Callaway County, Missouri, Illustrated* (St. Louis: National Historical Company, 1884), 94 (hereinafter cited as *Callaway, 1884*).

4. *Callaway, 1884*, 100–112, 159–60.

5. Ibid., 160, 413.

6. *Compendium of the Enumeration of the Inhabitants and Statistics of the United States as Obtained from Returns of the Sixth Census* (1841; rpt., New York: Arno Press, 1976), 311–13.

7. Ibid.; *Seventh Census of the United States, 1850, An Appendix* (1853; rpt., New York: Arno Press, 1976), 675–82 (hereinafter cited as *Appendix, 1850 Census*).

8. Phillip V. Scarpino, "Slavery in Callaway County, Missouri, 1845–1855," Part 1, *Missouri Historical Review 71* (October 1976): 27.

9. Ibid., 29.

10. *Callaway, 1884*, 187–90.

11. *Agricultural Schedules of the Seventh Census of the United States, 1850, Missouri. A to C* (Washington, D.C.: National Archives, 1963, microfilm), P. 343, roll 1 (hereinafter cited as *Agricultural Census, 1850*).

12. *Population Schedules of the Seventh Census of the United States, 1850, Missouri Slave Schedules, Adair County through*

Franklin County (Washington, D.C.: National Archives, 1963, microfilm), p. . 230, roll 422 (hereinafter cited as *1850 Slave Census*).

13. *1850 Callaway Census*, 393; *1876 Atlas of Missouri; Marriage Records of Callaway County, Missouri*, Fulton Public Library, Fulton, Mo.

14. *1850 Callaway Census*, 393; Hugh P. Williamson, "Document: The State of Missouri Against Celia, A Slave," *Midwest Journal* 8 (Spring/Fall 1956): 409.

15. *1850 Callaway Census*, 393; Testimony of James Coffee Waynescot in "State of Missouri Versus Celia, A Slave," Callaway County Court, October term, 1855, Callaway County courthouse, Fulton, Mo., file 4496 (hereinafter cited as Celia File 4496).

16. Testimony of Jefferson Jones, Celia File 4496.

17. *Appendix, 1850 Census*, 675–82; Scarpino, "Slavery in Callaway County," 26–29.

18. *Callaway, 1884*, 189, 190–94.

19. Ovid Bell, *A Short History of Callaway County* (N.p. 1933), 22–27.

20. *Missouri Republican* (St. Louis), August 15, 1855.

21. *Callaway, 1884*, 278–79, 437–38; Bell, *A Short History of Callaway County*, 19–20.

22. *1850 Slave Census*, 263; *Population Schedules of the Seventh Census of the United States, 1850, Missouri. Buchanan, Butler, Caldwell and Callaway Counties* (Washington, D. C.: National Archives, 1963, microfilm), p. 249, roll 393 (hereinafter cited as *1850 Census Population Schedules*).

23. *Callaway, 1884,* 278, 417–19; Bell, *A Short History of Callaway County,* 19–20.

24. *1850 Census Population Schedules, 249; Callaway, 1884, 279; Biographical Directory of the United States Congress, 1774–1989, Bicentennial Edition* (Washington, D. C.: Government Printing Office, 1989), 1255.

Two:
The Crime

1. Glover Moore, *The Missouri Controversy, 1819–1821* (Lexington: University Press of Kentucky, 1953), 339; also see Charles S. Sydnor, *The Development of Southern Sectionalism, 1819–1848* (Baton Rouge: Louisiana State University Press, 1948), 131. Moore's work remains the best survey of the Missouri crisis.

2. Moore, *The Missouri Controversy,* 258–73; Benjamin G. Merkel, "The Abolition Aspects of Missouri's Anti-Slavery Controversy, 1819–1865," *Missouri Historical Review* 44 (1950): 232–45.

3. Don E. Fehrenbacher, *The South and Three Sectional Crises* (Baton Rouge: Louisiana State University Press, 1980), 9–23.

4. Harrison A. Trexler, *Slavery in Missouri, 1804–1865* (Baltimore: Johns Hopkins University Press, 1914), 13–17; Phillip V. Scarpino, "Slavery in Callaway County, Missouri."

5. *1850 Slave Census,* 230.

6. *Appendix, 1850 Census,* 655.

7. Merkel, "Missouri's Anti-Slavery Controversy," 232–45; Hamilton Holman, *Prologue to Conflict: The Crisis and Compromise of 1850* (Lexington: University Press of Kentucky, 1964), 108–19; Avery O. Craven, *The Growth of Southern Nationalism, 1848–1861* (Baton Rouge: Louisiana State University Press, 1953), 177.

8. Testimony of Jefferson Jones, Celia File 4496; Darlene Clark Hine, "Rape and the Inner Lives of Black Women in the Middle West," *Signs* 14 (Summer 1989): 912; Elizabeth Fox-Genovese, *Within the Plantation Household: Black and White Women of the Old South* (Chapel Hill: University of North Carolina Press, 1988), 325–26; Deborah Gray White, *Ar'n't I a Woman: Female Slaves in the Plantation South* (New York: Norton, 1985), 26–46. Catherine Clinton's essay, "Caught in the Web of the Big House: Women and Slavery," in *The Web of Southern Relations: Women, Family and Education*, Walter J. Fraser, Jr., R. Frank Saunders, Jr., and Jon L. Wakelyn, eds. (Athens: University of Georgia Press, 1985), 19–34, provides an excellent brief summary of the manner in which historians have dealt with the sexual exploitation of female slaves. Also see Angela Davis, "Introduction," *Black Scholar* 3 (December 1971): 3–15.

9. Fogel, *Without Consent or Contract*, 180–81; Robert W. Fogel and Stanley L. Engerman, *Time on the Cross: The Economics of American Negro Slavery* (Boston: Little, Brown, 1974), 135–39; Paul D. Escott, *Slavery Remembered: A Record of Twentieth-Century Slave Narratives* (Chapel Hill: University of North Carolina Press, 1979), 52–53; John W. Blassingame, *The Slave Community: Plantation Life in the Ante-bellum South* (New York: Oxford University Press, 1972), 77–103.

10. See Ann W. Burgess and Lynda L. Holmstrom, *Rape, Crisis and Recovery* (Bowie, Md.: Robert J. Brady, 1979),

35–65; and Thomas W. McCahill, Linda C. Meyer, and Arthur M. Fischman, *The Aftermath of Rape* (Lexington, Mass.: Lexington Books, 1979), 23–79.

11. Two of the more recent works on the subject are Catherine Clinton, *The Plantation Mistress* (New York; Pantheon, 1982); and White, *Ar'n't I a Woman*, especially 27–46. Also see Jacqueline Jones, *Labor of Love, Labor of Sorrow* (New York: Basic Books, 1985), 24–28; Fox-Genovese, *Within the Plantation Household*, 325–26. Some black male slaves also evidently believed black females to "have a good deal of sexual passion," as indicated by the 1863 testimony of Robert Smalls to the American Freedmen's Inquiry Commission, in John W. Blassingame, ed., *Slave Testimony: Two Centuries of Letters, Speeches, Interviews and Autobiographies* (Baton Rouge: Louisiana State University Press, 1977), 374–77.

12. Orville Vernon Burton, *In My Father's House Are Many Mansions: Family and Community in Edgefield, South Carolina* (Chapel Hill: University of North Carolina Press, 1985), 185–89. For additional information on Hammond's sexual exploitation of his slaves, see Carol Bleser, *Secret and Sacred: The Diaries of James Henry Hammond, a Southern Slaveholder* (New York: Oxford University Press, 1988), 17–21, 212–13.

13. Escott, *Slavery Remembered*, 50–54; Herbert G. Gutman, *The Black Family in Slavery and Freedom, 1750–1925* (New York: Vintage, 1977), 267–303; Blassingame, *The Slave Community*, 87–89.

14. Jones, *Labor of Love*, 350–51; White, *Ar'n't I a Woman*, 152–53.

15. Letter of Harvey Newsom dated July 29, 1855, in *Missouri Republican*, August 2, 1855; testimony of William Powell and Virginia Waynescot, Celia File 4496.

16. Testimony of Jefferson Jones and William Powell, Celia File 4496; see also Clinton, *The Plantation Mistress*, chapter 11.

17. Blassingame, *The Slave Community*, 88–89; Fox-Genovese, *Within the Plantation Household*, 326–27.

18. Testimony of Jefferson Jones, Celia File 4496.

19. For discussions of female slave resistance, see Fox-Genovese, *Within the Plantation Household*, 290–333; White, *Ar'n't I a Woman*, 62–90.

20. Testimony of William Powell, Celia File 4496.

21. See Fox-Genovese, *Within the Plantation Household*, especially chaps. 5 and 7.

22. Testimony of William Powell and Virginia Waynescot, Celia File 4496; White, *Ar'n't I a Woman*, 27–46; Fox-Genovese, *Within the Plantation Household*, 242–89.

23. Testimony of Jefferson Jones, Celia File 4496. The complexity of a rapist's view of his victim is suggested by several studies. For example, in A. Nicholas Groth's *Men Who Rape: The Psychology of the Offender* (New York: Plenum Press, 1979), the author observes that a certain type of rapist, classified as a "power rapist," denies the forcible nature of his sexual encounter and "needs to feel that his victim needed and wanted and enjoyed it" (25–31). Another study of rapists finds that "protestations of love [for the victim] are quite common"; Lorenne M. G. Clark and Debra J. Lewis, *Rape: The Price of Coercive Sexuality* (Toronto: The Women's Press, 1977), 100–106.

24. Testimony of Jefferson Jones, Celia File 4496.

25. Testimony of Virginia and Coffee Waynescot, Celia File 4496.

26. Testimony of William Powell, Jefferson Jones, and Thomas Shoatman, Celia File 4496.

27. Ibid.

28. Testimony of Coffee Waynescot, Celia File 4496.

Three:
Inquisition

1. Testimony of Virginia Waynescot, Harry Newsom, and William Powell, Celia File 4496; *Callaway, 1884*, 697–98.

2. *Agricultural Census, 1850*, 345; *1850 Slave Census*, 230.

3. Inquest and trial testimony of William Powell, Celia File 4496.

4. Ibid.

5. Ibid.

6. Ibid.

7. Testimony of William Powell, Harry Newsom, and Virginia Waynescot, Celia File 4496.

8. Testimony of Virginia Waynescot, Celia File 4496.

9. *Callaway, 1884*, 159; *Agricultural Census, 1850*, 343; *1850 Census Population Schedules*, 197; Celia File 4496; Scarpino, "Slavery in Callaway County," part 1, 25.

10. Celia File 4496.

11. *1850 Slave Census*, 236; *1850 Census Population Schedules*, 202, 203, 212, 232, 239.

12. Inquest testimony of William Powell, Coffee Wayne-scot, and Celia, Celia File 4496; affidavits and summons, Celia File 4496.

13. Ibid.; inquest transcript, Celia File 4496.

14. Whyte and Howe to county court, June 25, 1855, Celia File 4496; various inquest documents, Celia File 4496.

15. Boonville *Weekly Observer*, July 7, 1855; *Missouri Republican*, June 28, 1855. While issues of the *Fulton Telegraph* for this period are not extant, other newspaper editors on occasion clipped and ran items from its pages.

16. Testimony of Jefferson Jones, Celia File 4496.

17. The most thorough account of the impact of the Haitian revolt upon the psyche of the white South is contained in Alfred N. Hunt, *Haiti's Influence on Antebellum America* (Baton Rouge: Louisiana State University Press, 1988), especially 114–39; Scarpino, "Slavery in Callaway County," part 2, 273. For a general overview of slave rebellions, Herbert Aptheker's *American Negro Slave Revolts* (New York; Columbia University Press, 1943), despite its faults, remains the place to start.

18. Of the many accounts of the Turner rebellion, perhaps the best, and certainly the most readable, is Stephen B. Oates's *The Fires of Jubilee: Nat Turner's Fierce Rebellion* (New York: Harper & Row, 1975).

19. Aptheker, *American Negro Slave Revolts*, 341–42; *Liberator*, August 24, 1855; *Missouri Republican*, June 27, July 17, 1855; *Dollar Missouri Journal*, June 21, 1855.

20. *Callaway, 1884*, 420–21.

21. Testimony of Jefferson Jones and Thomas Shoatman, Celia File 4496.

22. William S. Bryan and Robert Rose, *A History of Pioneer Families of Missouri* (St. Louis: Bryan, Brand, 1876), 426–28; *1850 Slave Census*, 263; *Population Schedules of the Eighth Census of the United States*, 1860. *Missouri Slave Schedules*, Vol. I (Washington, D. C.: National Archives, 1967, microfilm), p. 111, roll 653 (hereinafter cited as *1860 Slave Census*).

23. Testimony of Jefferson Jones, Celia File 4496.

24. *Missouri Republican,* August 2, 1855.

Four:
Backdrop

1. For an example of the *Telegraph*'s coverage of these events see the *Dollar Missouri Journal,* July 5, 1855.

2. Samuel A. Johnson, *The Battle Cry of Freedom: The New England Emigrant Aid Company in the Kansas Crusade* (Lawrence: University Press of Kansas, 1954), 7.

3. Ibid., 16–17, 65–71, 74–75.

4. Duane G. Meyer, *The Heritage of Missouri*, 3d ed. (St. Louis: River City, 1982), 336–39; Elmer L. Craik, *Southern Interest in Territorial Kansas, 1854–1858* (N.p., N.d. [rpt. from the Collections of the Kansas Historical Society, xv]), 345–47, 352–61; Lester B. Baltimore, "Benjamin F. Stringfellow: The Fight for Slavery on the Missouri Border," *Missouri Historical Review* 62 (October 1967): 14–29; Theodore C. Atchinson,

"David R. Atchinson," *Missouri Historical Review* 24 (July 1930): 502–15.

5. Johnson, *The Battle Cry of Freedom*, 98; Perry McCandless, *A History of Missouri*, Vol. 2, *1820–1860* (Columbia: University of Missouri Press, 1972), 264–68.

6. Meyer, *The Heritage of Missouri*, 337; Richard O. Boyer, *The Legend of John Brown: A Biography and History* (New York: Knopf, 1973), 496–97.

7. Roy V. Mayers, "The Raid on the *Parkville Industrial Luminary*," *Missouri Historical Review* 30 (October 1935): 39–46; David D. March, *The History of Missouri*, Vol. 2 (New York: Lewis, 1967), 843–45.

8. *Dollar Missouri Journal*, June 21, 1855.

9. Trexler, *Slavery in Missouri*, 199–202; *Missouri Republican*, June 27, July 2, 5, 9, 1855; *Daily Democrat*, July 7, 9, 1855. In general, St. Louis papers opposed the convention, as did the *Intelligencer* and the *Democrat*. So, too, did the Columbia *Statesman*. The *Missouri Republican*, on the other hand, was supportive.

10. David E. Harrell, Jr., "James Shannon: Preacher, Educator and Fire Eater," *Missouri Historical Review* 63 (January 1969): 135–70.

11. *Dollar Missouri Journal*, July 12, 19, 1855.

12. Ibid., July 27, 1855.

13. Floyd C. Shoemaker, "Missouri's Fight for Kansas, 1854–1855," *Missouri Historical Review* 48 July 1954): 335–38; *Daily Democrat*, July 19, 1855; *Missouri Republican*, July 16, 17, 1855.

14. Harrell, "James Shannon," 161–62.

15. *Missouri Republican*, July 17, 1855.

16. Ibid., July 16, 17, 19, 1855; *Dollar Missouri Journal*, July 19, 1855; *Daily Democrat*, July 19, 1855.

17. Harrell, "James Shannon," 161–62; Walter B. Davis and Daniel S. Durrie, *An Illustrated History of Missouri* (St. Louis: A. J. Hall, 1876), 142–43.

18. *Dollar Missouri Journal*, August 2, 1855.

19. *New York National Anti-Slavery Standard*, July 28, 1855; *Missouri Republican*, October 9, 1855; *Dollar Missouri Journal*, August 23, 1855; *Liberator*, July 6, 1855.

20. Johnson, *The Battle Cry of Freedom*, 102–3; James A. Rawley, *Race and Politics: "Bleeding Kansas" and the Coming of the Civil War* (Lincoln: University of Nebraska Press, 1969), 86–94; Lynda L. Crist, ed., *The Papers of Jefferson Davis*, Vol. 5, *1853–1855* (Baton Rouge: Louisiana State University Press, 1985), 446.

21. Johnson, *The Battle Cry of Freedom*, 106; Boyer, *The Legend of John Brown*, 504.

22. Rawley, *Race and Politics*, 94–95; Johnson, *The Battle Cry of Freedom*, 107–8; D. W. Wilder, *The Annals of Kansas, 1841–1885* (1886; rpt., New York: Arno Press, 1975), 75–77.

23. Wilder, *Annals of Kansas*, 78; Boyer, *The Legend of John Brown*, 557–71; Johnson, *The Battle Cry of Freedom*, 107–8; Rawley, *Race and Politics*, 94–96.

24. *Missouri Republican*, July 21, 1855.

Five:
The Trial

1. *Biographical Directory of Congress*, 1116.

2. *Liberator*, October 19, 1855.

3. Bell, *A Short History of Callaway County*, 19–20; *Callaway, 1884*, 278.

4. *Congressional Globe, 30th Cong.*, 1st sess., 1848, vol. 19, pp. 180–90, 1037; *Callaway, 1884*, 278–79; Bell, *A Short History of Callaway County*, 19–20.

5. *Callaway, 1884*, 279.

6. Ibid.

7. *1850 Census Population Schedules*, 539; *Callaway, 1884*, 188–90; *1850 Slave Census*, 184; Robert Walker, "Nathan Chapman Kouns," *Missouri Historical Review* 24 (July 1930), 516–20.

8. *1850 Census Population Schedules*, 438; *Agricultural Census, 1850*, 359; *Callaway, 1884*, 172.

9. *Callaway, 1884*, 627.

10. Ibid., 279; *Biographical Directory of Congress*, 1255.

11. David E. Harrell, Jr., *A Social History of the Disciples of Christ*, vol. I, *Quest for a Christian America: The Disciples of Christ and American Society to 1866* (Nashville: Disciples of Christ Historical Society, 1966), 91–138, 106.

12. Bryan and Rose, *Pioneer Families of Missouri*, 184; *Callaway, 1884*, 113; Trial record, Celia File 4496.

13. *Agricultural Census, 1850*, 361; *Callaway, 1884*, 255.

14. Williamson, "Document," 415.

15. Trial testimony, Celia File 4496; 1850 *Slave Census*, 106, 232, 241, 250; *1850 Census Population Schedules*, 200, 211, 216–17, 222–27, 283, 299.

16. Trial testimony, Celia File 4496.

17. Ibid.

18. Ibid.

19. Ibid.; "Jury Instructions" (Document O), Celia File 4496.

20. *Callaway, 1884*, 404; *1850 Slave Census*, 93.

21. Trial testimony, Celia File 4496.

22. Mark V. Tushnet, *The American Law of Slavery, 1810–1860* (Princeton: Princeton University Press, 1981), 108–39. Successful use of the argument of self-defense by slaves was rare, however. See Philip J. Schwarz, *Twice Condemned; Slaves and the Criminal Laws of Virginia, 1705–1865* (Baton Rouge: Louisiana State University Press, 1988), 240–41.

23. Trial testimony, Celia File 4496.

Six:
The Verdict

1. "Jury Instructions" (Document O), Celia File 4496.

2. *Revised Statutes of the State of Missouri, 1845* (St. Louis: Chambers and Knapp, 1845), art. 2, sec. 22, 573 (hereinafter

cited as *Missouri Statutes, 1845*). Also, see Trexler, *Slavery in Missouri*, 75–77.

3. "Jury Instructions" (Document O), Celia File 4496.

4. *Missouri Statutes, 1845*, art. 2, sec. 4, 180.

5. Even historians who refute charges that slaveholders systematically bred slaves note the economic significance of slave reproduction. Rather than directly interfering with their slaves' sexual lives, they contend, planters used "positive economic incentives" to "influence fertility patterns." Ironically, they use James Hammond's advice to an overseer to make their point. See Fogel and Engerman, *Time on the Cross*, 78–86. For less favorable views of slaveholders' efforts to influence fertility patterns, see Escott, *Slavery Remembered*, 44–45; White, *Ar'n't I a Woman*, 98–110.

6. "Jury Instructions" (Document O), Celia File 4496. The prosecution's insistence that the master's power could be resisted only if a slave's life were threatened had ample precedent in southern courts. For example, see the discussion of the North Carolina cases *State v. Mann* and *State v. Hoover* and the Mississippi case *State v. Isaac Jones* in Paul Finkelman, *The Law of Freedom and Bondage: A Casebook* (New York: Oceana, 1986), 217–30, 248–50.

7. "Jury Instructions" (Document O), Celia File 4496.

8. Ibid.

9. Lorenzo J. Greene, Gary Kremer, and Anthony F. Holland, *Missouri's Black Heritage* (St. Louis: Forum Press, 1980), 30; Eugene P. Genovese, *Roll, Jordan, Roll: The World the Slaves Made* (New York: Pantheon, 1972), 33. Phillips also acknowledged both that slave women were sexually assaulted and that such assaults were not considered rape, *American Negro Slavery* (New York: D. Appleton, 1918), 458.

10. Tushnet, *The American Law of Slavery*, 37–43.

11. Don E. Fehrenbacher, *The Dred Scott Case: Its Significance in American Law and Politics* (New York: Oxford University Press, 1978), 250–65, 322–34. For a thorough consideration of the manner in which slavery influenced concepts of comity within the American federal system, see Paul Finkelman, *An Imperfect Union: Slavery, Federalism and Comity* (Chapel Hill: University of North Carolina Press, 1981).

12. Fehrenbacher, *The Dred Scott Case*, 252–56, 392–93.

13. Fox-Genovese, *Within the Plantation Household*, 326–27.

14. Tushnet, *The American Law of Slavery*, 85–86; Finkelman, *The Law of Freedom and Bondage*, 260–61; Trexler, *Slavery in Missouri*, 73.

15. Helen T. Caterall, ed., *Judicial Cases Concerning American Slavery and the Negro*, 5 vols. (1926; rpt., New York: Negro University Press, 1968). For representative state studies see Orville Taylor, *Negro Slavery in Arkansas* (Durham: Duke University Press, 1958), 232–35; James B. Sellers, *Slavery in Alabama* (University: University of Alabama Press, 1950), 215–65; and Trexler, *Slavery in Missouri*, 73. Also see the Missouri section of George P. Rawick, ed., *The American Slave: A Composite Autobiography*, vol. 11, *Arkansas Narratives, Part 7 and Missouri Narratives* (Westport, Conn: Greenwood, 1972). Yet another study to fail to consider the rape of slave women is Robert W. Duffner, "Slavery in Missouri River Counties, 1820–1865" (Ph.D. dissertation, University of Missouri, 1974), 64–67, 110–112.

16. Schwarz, *Twice Condemned*, 159–61.

17. Ibid. Other recent historians, including women, continue to ignore the problem of the rape of slave women. For an example, see Fox-Genovese, *Within the Plantation Household*, 235–41. This omission is accounted for in part by Fox-Genovese's contention that in a system that gave white males absolute power slave women "sought, not virtue, but triumph." Virtue could be defended only after freedom had been achieved, 396.

18. See, for example, Dorothy Sterling, ed., *We Are Your Sisters: Black Women in the Nineteenth Century* (New York: Norton, 1984), 18–31; Hine, "Rape and the Inner Lives of Black Women," 912; Jean Fagan Yellin, "The Text and Contexts of Harriet Jacobs' *Incidents in the Life of a Slave Girl: Written by Herself*," in Charles T. Davis and Henry Louis Gates, Jr., eds., *The Slave's Narrative* (Oxford: Oxford University Press, 1985), 262–82.

19. William K. Scarborough, *The Overseer: Plantation Management in the Old South* (Baton Rouge: Louisiana State University Press, 1966), 75–77. Scarborough observes that planters "universally discouraged" their overseers from having sexual relations with female slaves. Yet in language that implies that female slaves were responsible for such relationships, he notes that some overseers ignored instructions and entered into sexual relationships "with sirens of the slave quarter."

20. For a good brief summary of the way in which historians have dealt with the sexual exploitation of female slaves, see Clinton, "Caught in the Web of the Big House," 19–34. On the subject in the WPA slave narratives, see Escott, *Slavery Remembered*, 46. David Bradley, *The Chaneysville Incident* (New York: Harper & Row, 1981) illustrates the use of the theme in the work of current black male fiction writers. Toni Morrison, *Beloved: A Novel* (New York: Knopf, 1987), is a

powerful treatment of the theme by one of the United States' foremost novelists. Sherley Anne Williams, *Dessa Rose* (New York: Morrow, 1986), also explores the theme of interracial sex in the Old South. The character Dessa Rose resembles Celia, although based on another incident, and meets a happier, if historically inaccurate, fate. Also, for an exploration of the theme in a memoir, see Pauli Murray, *Proud Shoes: The Story of an American Family* (New York: Harper & Row, 1956), 33–44.

21. Fox-Genovese, *Within the Plantation Household*, chaps. 4 and 5, especially pages 195 and 241.

22. The definitive study of the southern code of honor is Bertram Wyatt-Brown, *Southern Honor, Ethics and Behavior in the Old South* (Oxford: Oxford University Press, 1982), especially 117–49, 226–92. Also see Fox-Genovese, *Within the Plantation Household*, 63–64, 101–2. For an excellent planter's summary of his role as patriarch, see James O. Breeden, ed., *Advice Among Masters: The Ideal in Slave Management in the Old South* (Westport, Conn: Greenwood, 1980), 59.

23. Trial record and jury verdict, Celia File 4496.

24. Trial record, Celia File 4496.

25. Ibid.

26. Testimony of William Powell and Virginia Waynescot, Celia File 4496; "Bill of Cash in the Case of Celia, a Slave" (Document G-1), Celia File 4496; *Missouri Statutes, 1845*, art. 6, sec. 18, 463.

27. Williamson, "Document," 418; Trial record, Celia File 4496.

Seven:
Final Disposition

1. Jameson, Boulware, and Kouns to Abiel Leonard, December 6, 1855, Celia File 4496.

2. *Dollar Missouri Journal,* November 17, 1855.

3. Jameson, Boulware, and Kouns to Abiel Leonard, December 6, 1855, Celia File 4496.

4. Ibid.

5. Rawley, *Race and Politics,* 95–96; Johnson, *The Battle Cry of Freedom,* 108–9; Wilder, *Annals of Kansas,* 84–86, 91–106.

6. For examples, see *Daily Missouri Democrat,* November 13, 17, 1855; *Missouri Republican,* November 1, 1855.

7. Johnson, *The Battle Cry of Freedom,* 109–10; Rawley, *Race and Politics,* 96; *Daily Democrat,* November 28, December 5, 1855.

8. Wilder, *Annals of Kansas,* 87; Rawley, *Race and Politics,* 96–97.

9. *Daily Democrat,* December 25, 1855; *Dollar Missouri Journal,* December 13, 1855; Wilder, *Annals of Kansas,* 87.

10. *Missouri Republican,* December 25, 1855; *Dollar Missouri Journal,* December 13, 1855; *Daily Democrat,* December 24, 25, 1855.

11. Wilder, *Annals of Kansas,* 87–88; Johnson, *The Battle Cry of Freedom,* 138–43; *Daily Democrat,* December 20, 22, 24, 25, 1855; *Missouri Republican,* December 1, 4, 19, 21, 24, 1855.

12. Davis and Durrie, *An Illustrated History of Missouri*, 142–43; McCandless, *A History of Missouri*, 2: 267–68.

13. Fehrenbacher, *The Dred Scott Case*, 263–65.

14. Frederick A. Culmer, "Abiel Leonard," parts 4, 5, *Missouri Historical Review* 28 (October 1933, January 1934), 17–37, 103–24.

15. Document II-1, Celia File 4496.

16. *Fulton Telegraph*, January 4, 1856, as quoted in the *New York Times*, January 16, 1856.

17. Document G-1, "Bill of Cash," Celia File 4496.

18. *1860 Slave Census*, 104.

Eight:
Conclusions

1. Hine, "Rape and the Inner Lives of Black Women," 912–13.

2. Stanley Elkins, *Slavery: A Problem in American Institutional and Intellectual Life*, 3d ed. (Chicago: University of Chicago Press, 1976). Originally published in 1959, Elkins's work, which compares slavery to the Nazi death camps, drew spirited criticism and prompted historians to examine more thoroughly the social organization of the slave community. See, for example, Blassingame, *The Slave Community*. However, it must be noted that even though Blassingame contends that the "typical slave . . . preserved his manhood in the quarters,

he also notes that "the most serious impediment to the [slave] man's acquisition of status in his family was his inability to protect his wife from the sexual advances of whites and the physical abuse of his master," (216, 82–88).

3. Fox-Genovese, *Within the Plantation Household*, 308–33, 372–96; Harriet A. Jacobs, *Incidents in the Life of a Slave Girl, Written by Herself*, edited by Jean Fagan Yellin (Cambridge, Mass.: Harvard University Press, 1987).

4. Alice Walker, *The Color Purple* (New York: Harcourt, Brace, Jovanovich, 1982).

5. Most recent studies of slavery reflect the work of Blassingame and Gutman, and stress the ability of slaves to resist the constraints of slavery and develop their own social institutions. Among them are Burton, *In My Father's House Are Many Mansions*, especially chapter 4; and Fogel and Engerman, *Time on the Cross*, 126–44, 242–43. Fogel notes the many factors that have led historians to disagree about the nature of the slave family in *Without Consent or Contract* and places additional stress on the moral problems of slavery (162–86, 394–95).

6. Genovese, *Roll, Jordan, Roll*, 25–49. Also see Kenneth M. Stampp, *The Peculiar Institution: Slavery in the Ante-Bellum South* (New York: Vintage, 1956), 192–237. Alan Watson's *Slave Law in the Americas* (Athens: University of Georgia Press, 1989) contends that racism and the fact that the southern states did not base their slave codes upon Roman law combined to make slave law more stringent in the United States, especially in the area that Watson calls "public law" (65–82). Of special interest is Watson's contention that in the South "fixed penalties to be inflicted on slaves by the owners had to be laid down simply because the state did not trust the owner to punish some slaves to the extent that the legislature considered sufficient" (128).

7. Tushnet, *The American Law of Slavery*, 30–37; Phillips, *American Negro Slavery*, 458. Schwarz, in *Twice Condemned*, 315–18, presents a non-Marxist interpretation that sees racism and fear of black violence as the more significant factors underlying slave law. Watson's *Slave Law,* on the other hand, stresses the role of the judiciary in shaping slave law, though he also emphasizes the role of racism, especially in the United States.

8. Genovese, *Roll, Jordan, Roll*, 25–70; Clarence L. Mohr, *On the Threshold of Freedom: Masters and Slaves in Civil War Georgia* (Athens: University of Georgia Press, 1986), summarizes reformers' efforts in antebellum Georgia (235–71).

9. Fogel, *Without Consent or Contract*, 394.

10. For an excellent review of the historiographical debate over the degree to which southerners were troubled by the morality of slavery, see Gaines M. Foster, "Guilt Over Slavery: An Historiographical Analysis," *Journal of Southern History* 56 (November 1990), 665–94. Foster concludes that it is impossible to prove or disprove the "guilt thesis," that southerners felt guilty because of slavery. He contends that recent historians have noted that southerners' "doubt and confusion" about slavery resulted from "contradictions inherent in the institution. . . ." This approach, Foster contends, "does minimize the psychological turmoil with which southern modernists invested the Old South, and reduces their sense of the region's uniqueness rooted in guilt," 692–94. Foster, however, does not explore the moral nature of the intensely personal decisions slavery forced southerners to make, as the case of Celia demonstrates. Nor does he explain why, if southerners were convinced that slavery was morally acceptable, they feared their slaves and took seriously the potential for slave revolts.

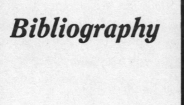

Bibliography

W hat follows is not intended as a comprehensive bibliography of scholarship on slavery or of a specific aspect of that institution. Indeed, so vast is the literature on slavery that comprehensive bibliographies treating either the economic or social aspects of slavery would increase the size of this volume considerably. Rather, what is provided here is a list of those documents, newspapers, and census materials from which this work was drawn, in addition to those secondary sources, books, and articles that were most frequently consulted.

Primary Sources

DOCUMENTS

Agricultural Schedules of the Seventh Census of the United States, 1850, Missouri, A to C. Washington, D.C.: National Archives, 1963. Microfilm. Roll 1.

Biographical Directory of the United States Congress, 1774–1989,

Bicentennial Edition. Washington, D.C.: Government Printing Office, 1989.

Compendium of the Enumeration of the Inhabitants and Statistics of the United States as Obtained from Returns of the Sixth Census. 1841. Reprint. New York: Arno Press, 1976.

Congressional Globe. 30th Cong., 1st Sess., 1848. Vol. 19.

1850 Federal Census for Callaway County, Missouri, Abstract. Compiled by Elizabeth P. Ellsberry. Missouri Department of Archives and History, Jefferson City, Mo.

1876 Atlas of Missouri; Marriage Records of Callaway County, Missouri. Fulton Public Library, Fulton, Mo.

Population Schedules of the Seventh Census of the United States, 1850, Missouri. Buchanan, Butler, Caldwell and Callaway Counties. Washington, D.C.: National Archives, 1963. Microfilm. Roll 393.

Population Schedules of the Seventh Census of the United States, 1850, Missouri Slave Schedules. Adair County through Franklin County. Washington, D.C.: National Archives, 1963. Microfilm. Roll 422.

Population Schedules of the Eighth Census of the United States, 1860. Missouri Slave Schedules. Vol. 1. Washington, D.C.: National Archives, 1967. Microfilm. Roll 653.

Revised Statutes of the State of Missouri, 1845. St. Louis: Chambers and Knapp, 1845.

Seventh Census of the United States, 1850, An Appendix. 1853. Reprint. New York: Arno Press, 1976.

State of Missouri versus Celia, a Slave. File 4496, Callaway County Court, October Term, 1855. Callaway County Courthouse, Fulton, Mo.

NEWSPAPERS

Daily Democrat (St. Louis).

Dollar Missouri Journal (Boonville and Columbia, Mo.)

Examiner (Jefferson City, Mo.)

Intelligencer (St. Louis, Mo.)
Liberator (Boston)
Missouri Republican (St. Louis)
New York National Anti-Slavery Standard
New York Times
Southwest Democrat (Jefferson City, Mo.)
Statesman (Columbia, Mo.)
Weekly Observer (Boonville, Mo.)

Secondary Sources

ARTICLES

Atchinson, Theodore C. "David R. Atchinson." *Missouri Historical Review* 24 July 1930): 502–15.

Baltimore, Lester B. "Benjamin F. Stringfellow: The Fight for Slavery on the Missouri Border." *Missouri Historical Review* 62 (October 1967): 14–29.

Clinton, Catherine. "Caught in the Web of the Big House: Women and Slavery." in *The Web of Southern Relations: Women, Family and Education*, Walter J. Fraser, Jr., R. Frank Saunders, Jr., and Jon L. Wakelyn, eds., 19–34. Athens: University of Georgia Press, 1985.

Culmer, Frederic A. "Abiel Leonard." Parts 4, 5. *Missouri Historical Review* 28 (October 1933, January 1934): 17–37, 103–24.

Davis, Angela. "Introduction." *Black Scholar* 3 (December 1971): 3–15.

Foster, Gaines M. "Guilt Over Slavery: A Historiographical Analysis." *Journal of Southern History* 56 (November 1990): 665–94.

Harrell, David E., Jr. "James Shannon: Preacher, Educator and Fire Eater." *Missouri Historical Review* 63 (January 1969): 135–70.

Hine, Darlene Clark. "Rape and the Inner Lives of Black Women in the Middle West." *Signs* 14 (Summer 1989): 912–20.

Mayers, Roy V. "The Raid on the *Parkville Industrial Luminary*." *Missouri Historical Review* 30 (October 1935): 39–46.

Merkel, Benjamin G. "The Abolition Aspects of Missouri's Anti-Slavery Controversy, 1819–1865." *Missouri Historical Review* 44 (1950): 232–45.

Oberholzer, Emil. "The Legal Aspects of Slavery in Missouri." Parts 1–4. *Bulletin of the Missouri Historical Society* 6 (January, April 1950): 139–61, 337–52.

Scarpino, Phillip V. "Slavery in Callaway County, Missouri, 1845–1855." Parts 1, 2. *Missouri Historical Review* 71 (October 1976, April 1977): 22–43, 266–83.

Sellers, Charles G., Jr. "The Travail of Slavery." In *The Southerner as American*, Charles G. Sellers, Jr., ed., 40–71. Chapel Hill: University of North Carolina Press, 1960.

Shoemaker, Floyd C. "Missouri's Fight for Kansas, 1854–55." *Missouri Historical Review* 48 (April, July 1954): 221–36, 325–40.

Walker, Robert. "Nathan Chapman Kouns." *Missouri Historical Review* 24 (July 1930): 516–20.

Williamson, Hugh P. "Document: The State of Missouri Against Celia, A Slave." *Midwest Journal* 8 (Spring/Fall 1956): 408–20.

Yellin, Jean Fagan. "The Text and Contexts of Harriet Jacobs' *Incidents in the Life of a Slave Girl: Written by Herself*," in *The Slave's Narrative*, Charles T. Davis and Henry Louis Gates, Jr., eds. 262–82. Oxford: Oxford University Press, 1985.

BOOKS

Aptheker, Herbert. *American Negro Slave Revolts*. New York: Columbia University Press, 1943.

Bell, Ovid. *A Short History of Callaway County.* N.p., 1933.

Blassingame, John W. *The Slave Community: Plantation Life in the Ante-bellum South.* New York; Oxford University Press, 1972.

Blassingame, John W., ed. *Slave Testimony: Two Centuries of Letters, Speeches, Interviews and Autobiographies.* Baton Rouge: Louisiana State University Press, 1977.

Bleser, Carol. *Secret and Sacred: The Diaries of James Henry Hammond, a Southern Slaveholder.* New York: Oxford University Press, 1988.

Boyer, Richard O. *The Legend of John Brown: A Biography and History.* New York: Knopf, 1973.

Bradley, David. *The Chaneysville Incident.* New York: Harper & Row, 1981.

Breeden, James O., ed. *Advice Among Masters: The ideal in Slave Management in the Old South.* Westport, Conn.: Greenwood, 1980.

Bryan, William S., and Robert Rose. *A History of Pioneer Families of Missouri.* St. Louis: Brand, 1876.

Burgess, Ann W., and Lynda L. Holmstrom. *Rape, Crisis and Recovery.* Bowie, Md.: Robert J. Brady, 1979.

Burton, Orville Vernon. *In My Father's House Are Many Mansions: Family and Community in Edgefield, South Carolina.* Chapel Hill: University of North Carolina Press, 1985.

Caterall, Helen T., ed. *Judicial Cases Concerning American Slavery and the Negro.* 5 vols. 1926. Reprint. New York: Negro University Press, 1968.

Clark, Lorenne M. G., and Debra J. Lewis. *Rape: The Price of Coercive Sexuality.* Toronto: Women's Press, 1977.

Clinton, Catherine. *The Plantation Mistress.* New York: Pantheon, 1982.

Craik, Elmer L. *Southern Interest in Territorial Kansas, 1854–1858.* Kansas Historical Society, XV. Reprint. N.p., n.d.

Craven, Avery O. *The Growth of Southern Nationalism, 1848–1861.* Baton Rouge: Louisiana State University Press, 1953.

Crist, Lynda L., ed. *The Papers of Jefferson Davis.* Vol. 5, *1853–1855.* Baton Rouge: Louisiana State University Press, 1985.

Davis, Walter B., and Daniel S. Durrie. *An Illustrated History of Missouri.* St. Louis: A. J. Hall, 1876.

Duffner, Robert W. "Slavery in Missouri River Counties, 1820–1865." Ph.D. dissertation, University of Missouri, 1974.

Elkins, Stanley. *Slavery: A Problem in American Institutional and Intellectual Life.* 3d ed. Chicago: University of Chicago Press, 1976.

Escott, Paul D. *Slavery Remembered: A Record of Twentieth-Century Slave Narratives.* Chapel Hill: University of North Carolina Press, 1979.

Fehrenbacher, Don E. *The Dred Scott Case: Its Significance in American Law and Politics.* New York: Oxford University Press, 1978.

———. *The South and Three Sectional Crises.* Baton Rouge: Louisiana State University Press, 1980.

Finkelman, Paul. *An Imperfect Union: Slavery, Federalism and Comity.* Chapel Hill: University of North Carolina Press, 1981.

———. *The Law of Freedom and Bondage: A Casebook.* New York: Oceana, 1986.

Fogel, Robert W. *Without Consent or Contract: The Rise and Fall of American Slavery.* New York: Norton, 1989.

Fogel, Robert W., and Stanley L. Engerman. *Time on the Cross: The Economics of American Negro Slavery.* Boston: Little, Brown, 1974.

Fox-Genovese, Elizabeth. *Within the Plantation Household: Black and White Women of the Old South.* Chapel Hill: University of North Carolina Press, 1988.

Genovese, Eugene P. *Roll, Jordan, Roll: The World the Slaves Made.* New York: Pantheon, 1972.

Greene, Lorenzo J., Gary Kremer, and Anthony F. Holland. *Missouri's Black Heritage.* St. Louis: Forum Press, 1980.

Groth, A. Nicholas. *Men Who Rape: The Psychology of the Offender.* New York: Plenum Press, 1979.

Gutman, Herbert G. *The Black Family in Slavery and Freedom, 1750–1925.* New York: Vintage, 1977.

Harrell, David E., Jr. *A Social History of the Disciples of Christ.* Vol. 1, *Quest for a Christian America: The Disciples of Christ and American Society to 1866.* Nashville: Disciples of Christ Historical Society, 1966.

History of Callaway County, Missouri, Illustrated. St. Louis: National Historical Company, 1884.

History of Callaway County, Missouri, 1984. Fulton, Mo.: Kingdom of Callaway Historical Society, 1983.

Holman, Hamilton. *Prologue to Conflict: The Crisis and Compromise of 1850.* Lexington: University Press of Kentucky, 1964.

Hunt, Alfred N. *Haiti's Influence on Antebellum America.* Baton Rouge: Louisiana State University Press, 1988.

Jacobs, Harriet A. *Incidents in the Life of a Slave Girl, Written by Herself.* Edited by Jean Fagan Yellin. Cambridge, Mass.: Harvard University Press, 1987.

Johnson, Samuel A. *The Battle Cry of Freedom: The New England Emigrant Aid Company in the Kansas Crusade.* Lawrence: University Press of Kansas, 1954.

Jones, Jacqueline. *Labor of Love, Labor of Sorrow.* New York: Basic Books, 1985.

McCahill, Thomas W., Linda C. Meyer, and Arthur M. Fischman. *The Aftermath of Rape.* Lexington, Mass.: Lexington Books, 1979.

McCandless, Perry. *A History of Missouri*. Vol. 2, *1820–1860*. Columbia: University of Missouri Press, 1972.

March, David D. *The History of Missouri*. Vol. 2. New York: Lewis, 1967.

Meyer, Duane G. *The Heritage of Missouri*. 3d ed. St. Louis: River City, 1982.

Mohr, Clarence L. *On the Threshold of Freedom: Masters and Slaves in Civil War Georgia*. Athens: University of Georgia Press, 1986.

Moore, Glover. *The Missouri Controversy, 1819–1821*. Lexington: University Press of Kentucky, 1953.

Morrison, Toni. *Beloved: A Novel*. New York: Knopf, 1987.

Murray, Pauli. *Proud Shoes: The Story of an American Family*. New York: Harper & Row, 1956.

Oates, Stephen B. *The Fires of Jubilee: Nat Turner's Fierce Rebellion*. New York: Harper & Row, 1975.

Phillips, Ulrich B. *American Negro Slavery*. New York: D. Appleton, 1918.

Rawick, George P., ed. *The American Slave: A Composite Autobiography*. Vol. 11, *Arkansas Narratives, Part 7 and Missouri Narratives*. Westport, Conn.: Greenwood, 1972.

Rawley, James A. *Race and Politics: "Bleeding Kansas" and the Coming of the Civil War*. Lincoln: University of Nebraska Press, 1969.

Scarborough, William K. *The Overseer: Plantation Management in the Old South*. Baton Rouge: Louisiana State University Press, 1966.

Schwarz, Philip J. *Twice Condemned: Slaves and the Criminal Laws of Virginia, 1705–1865*. Baton Rouge: Louisiana State University Press, 1988.

Sellers, James B. *Slavery in Alabama*. University: University of Alabama Press, 1950.

Stampp, Kenneth M. *The Peculiar Institution: Slavery in the Ante-Bellum South*. New York: Vintage, 1956.

Sterling, Dorothy, ed. *We Are Your Sisters: Black Women in the Nineteenth Century.* New York: Norton, 1984.

Sydnor, Charles S. *The Development of Southern Sectionalism, 1819–1848.* Baton Rouge: Louisiana State University Press, 1948.

Taylor, Orville. *Negro Slavery in Arkansas.* Durham: Duke University Press, 1958.

Trexler, Harrison A. *Slavery in Missouri, 1804–1865.* Baltimore: Johns Hopkins University Press, 1914.

Tushnet, Mark V. *The American Law of Slavery, 1810–1860.* Princeton: Princeton University Press, 1981.

Vestal, Stanley. *The Missouri.* New York & Toronto: Farrar & Rinehart, 1945.

Walker, Alice. *The Color Purple.* New York: Harcourt, Brace, Jovanovich, 1982.

Watson, Alan. *Slave Law in the Americas.* Athens: University of Georgia Press, 1989.

White, Deborah Gray. *Ar'n't I a Woman: Female Slaves in the Plantation South.* New York: Norton, 1985.

Wilder, D. W. *The Annals of Kansas, 1841–1885.* 1886. Reprint. New York: Arno Press, 1975.

Williams, Sherley Anne. *Dessa Rose.* New York: Morrow, 1986.

Wyatt-Brown, Bertram. *Southern Honor, Ethics and Behavior in the Old South.* Oxford: Oxford University Press, 1982.

Index

Index

178